West Memphis Witch Hunt

Poems supporting the WM3 defense

West Memphis Witch Hunt

Collected and edited
By
Misti Rainwater-Lites
&
Michael W. Johnson

Lulu press

ISBN 978-0-6151-5799-3

West Memphis Witch Hunt
Poems supporting the WM3 defense
© **2007**
All Rights Reserved.

Collected by Edited by:
Misti Rainwater-Lites
&
Michael W. Johnson

Designed by:
Michael W. Johnson

Front cover :   © 2007
By : James C. Coffelt   used with permission

Back cover :   © 2007
By: Michael McMahan   used with permission

ISBN 978-0-6151-5799-3 provided by:
Victor Schwartzman

TABLE OF CONTENTS

Intro   *page*7

Authors   *page*

TABLE OF CONTENTS

Authors — page

Small towns and superstitions…. makes me think of that "Love and Marriage" song that says, "You can't have one without the other". Since early civilization, it's been human nature to reject what is foreign and unknown. This is nothing novel. History has shown what cruelty can be inflicted when poised outside the confines of conformity.

Many have evolved past the primitive naïve views and can discern these monstrosities that have been enraptured in textbooks and stories worldwide as tragic, desolate periods of human era. War, famine, medieval monarchal reign, nazis and other supremacists, and the Salem witch trials can all be viewed in hindsight as dark chapters where radical extremist decisions were made that were not in the best interest of humanity.

Today in the southern aspect of the United States, among other areas, many stigmatisms and old-fashioned traditional taboos still hold a powerful validity over the land. Certain people cling to expired notions and ideals, thus halting the progress of cultural advancement. When it comes to right and wrong, they visualize only black and white with no gray possibilities.

When something catastrophic and unthinkable happens and a martyr is needed, they start searching immediately for those with opposing viewpoints and lifestyles. I know, for this happen to me. In no way does this compare to the adversities felt by the WM3 and others, but it is my own little tale of discrimination. Many years ago, my roommate and I were accused of spray-painting satanic and phallic images on two local churches in my hometown. We were harassed by cops for months and were told that all this evidence was pointing toward us and that we would be prosecuted for felony charges. I really thought that we would be taken to jail eventually. We never went. They finally stopped hounding us when they realized that we weren't going to own up to a crime we didn't commit. (In classic cop tricks, a cop told my friend that I had already admitted that he did it and that he should turn himself in; he didn't fall for it). Now why were we the prime suspects? It was because we were different than the majority. We were the outsiders who played rock and roll and didn't attend church with the masses.

This anthology of poetry has been brought together to raise more awareness and continue the fight against the unfortunate injustice that Damien, Jason, and Jessie continue to endure. Their story is a modern day witch hunt and is unbelievable, except that it is true. This could happen anywhere…to anyone. You could become a scapegoat for fear. We have come together as a collective voice to say that we will not tolerate this kind of prejudice and delinquency.

If you want more information on Damien, Jason, and Jessie, check out these sources:
www.wm3.org
"Paradise Lost" and "Paradise Lost 2 : Revelations" on DVD or VHS
"Devil's Knot" book by Mara Leveritt

I want to thank Misti Rainwater-Lites for conceiving this project and for caring about reversing the corrupt judicial actions taken against the WM3.
Thanks to Victor Schwartzman for being deeply concerned with the fate of the WM3 and for generously providing monetary assistance in the distribution of this book.
Thanks to the artists and poets who really got behind this anthology and contributed their artistic opinions.
And of course, thanks to Jessie, Jason, and Damien for being very brave and inspiring us all with their courage and perseverance.
Thanks for reading.

Michael W. Johnson

Jack T. Marlowe

Jack T. Marlowe is a writer of poetry and fiction.
A native of Dallas, Texas, he is founder and host
of the "Outlaws of the Spoken Word" open mic.
You can find Jack online at: www.inkandblood.net

voir dire (to speak the truth)

i empty my pockets
and wait in line
for my turn
to pass through
the metal detector
like last night's dinner
trying to navigate
a blocked intestine

onward
through the bowels
of the courthouse
catching a whiff
of someone's freedom
about to get shit on

the smell
of justice denied
of justice applied
by black-robed priests
of the law, by attorneys
like televangelists
or prosecuting salesmen
making their pitches

filling
the dockets
lawyers' pockets
prison cells
graves
and courtrooms

echoing
with kangaroo lies
and forced confessions
official oppression
marking
another notch
in the bench
another public intox
another murder rap

keeping the score
for blue suited pimps
profiting
from prostitution
and traffic tickets
while thorny thickets
of legalese ensnare
the unwary

the poor
the middle class
those too busy
working
to figure out
how to work
the system

victims
of corruption
bleeding
in the greedy jaws
of political expediency

guilty until found
innocent
but only found
innocent

are the lucky ones
the fortunate
sons of wealth
and power.

and meanwhile
in the central jury room
i hear a slurping sound
like someone sucking
the head of a cold beer

and i realize
the sound is coming
from two rows
in front of me

where
an old man
is asleep

asleep
and snoring
loudly

the unwitting
embodiment
of a nation
that
SERIOUSLY
NEEDS TO
FUCKING
WAKE UP.

~Jack T. Marlowe

the puppetmasters

the history books are full

the graveyards are full

the many hells are full
of puppetmasters
who could not
master themselves.

in death, they all discover
that they, too, have a master.

~Jack T. Marlowe

west memphis haiku

Arkansas witch trial:
a prosecutor plays God
but can't hide his horns

~Jack T. Marlowe

Leopold McGinnis

Leopold McGinnis has been published in enough places
(usually of ill-repute) to find writing new bios bothersome. He
is the founding editor of the online digizine www.redfez.net,
publishing under-appreciated, under-published authors from
across the universe.
Leopold has written and independently published a novel
(Game Quest)
and two novellas (The Red Fez and Bad Attitude). The last
thing in the world he ever thought he'd be was a poet, and often
wonders where he went wrong that he didn't end up in a
profession involving more (or any!) casual sex with gorgeous
women and frequent shooting of laser-guns.

Candide's Garden

You only need to pay people
To do what they won't do for free
To do things they don't consider
worthwhile enough to do
without some sort of payback.

So what sort of payback
are we reaping
In a world where everything
Is about payback?
Planting towering glass gardens that block the sun
Cash crops of
assembly lines of workers
Row by row,
methodological icons toiling in
the fascist's dream of a metal farm
A million identical carrots
piercing through the earth
cut and pasted across the landscape of our
inner space
while we let our loves, interests, dreams
wither and die

Paradoxically…
what is too important to wait for money
becomes not important enough to do for money
becomes unimportant
becomes a stale dream
beyond the reach of our finger tips
A false dream
told by our parents' parents' parents

Voltaire said the only way to survive
was to tend your own garden.
Candide,
What has happened to our gardens?

~ Leopold McGinnis

Sapper

Your cloud world lives
On a puff of steam
The only thing holding it up
Is the fact that people can't see
Through the mist
Only the power of belief
Floating high over reason
Keeps this
Self-promotional
Back-scratching
Empire of incest hovering above
The nuclear spit
Of your engines

But I'm down here
In the wasteland
And one by one I'm knocking out the pillars
And one day
Before you know it
Your whole empire will crumble
And here we'll all be
Back on the ground again.

~ Leopold McGinnis

Relentless

Relentless
Like an abusive father
this world will teach you
with its fists
Beat your spirit
until you submit
say you're sorry
learn the lessons it taught you
and turn them on the next dog
snarling, gnashing teethfights
in back alleys
Pound for pound
It gave you your flesh
And it can, it will take it back
In blood or in service
If there's fight left
you can embrace defeat
welcome the inevitable
let the thunder rain
upon your skin
Striking you deeper
And deeper
into the ground
 From whence you
Sprung
Until you lie down
like a dog
Until you lie down
like Kafka
And die.

~ Leopold McGinnis

Theron Moore

Theron Moore is the co-editor of St. Vitus Press.
http://www.saintvituspress.com/

THEY WAS KILLIN' PEOPLE DOWN BY THE RIVER

"They was killin' people down by the river"
was what the townsfolk was sayin'
to the tv people and reporters
who'd been sniffin' 'round
these parts this past week
when three local kids
went missin' last Friday
then turned up dead
down by the river's edge
even had a few folks say they saw
an old 70's boogie van
cruising' 'round town last week
an' parked over by the local school
but paid no more mind to it
than anything else
since this is a tourist town
had three kids found by the
side of the river on Sunday morn
hacked up
disfigured
and violated
a damn shame and certainly a tragedy
for a town as quiet and small as this
the cops say they spotted a van
the next county over that met
the description of that strange
and mysterious boogie van
that's got the whole town buzzin'
but nothin' ever became of it
which makes sense considering
the fact that I have that beast
locked up tight in my garage
bloodstains and all
I figure someday I'll wash her
but for now

I like to sit inside her
with my headphones on
listening to death metal
reliving their screams in my head
over and over and over again
what can I say man
these are violent times
we live in

~Theron Moore

BUM FUCK

Just another bum
that's gotta choose or lose
between pussy and food
which meant
another night
without soup
nor drink
gonna curl up
in garbage bags
and sniff my dinner
hair by hair
off my mustache
and beard
till I find another
frozen stiff
I can lick off
and finger
then rob
before the
pigs catch
up to me

~Theron Moore

MY OWN PERSONAL MURDER

I heard her…
coupla bar stools over…
clickety clack, clickety clack
against her wine glass
a real Anna Nicole type
that had been rode hard
most of her life
those long finger nails
spellin' out the story
of her wasted life
painted bright pink
speakin' in her southern drawl
that drew everyone in
around her and then some
"I'm just boozy, druggy
more pills than booze"
she said, slurring
at the bartender, talking to
anyone who would listen
unfortunately I heard
everything she said
and began imagining
her dead and embalmed
lying pretty in her casket
on a crisp Saturday morning
the next Black Dahlia
my next artistic project
my own personal murder
clock strikes 2 AM
as I get myself ready
to join her
for the ultimate
last call

~Theron Moore   *23*

Kaveh Akbar

Kaveh Akbar is a tall poet living in a small Indiana town. He is editor of the for-charity zine *The Quirk*. He has placed poems in *Poesy, remark.*, *Poems-For-All*, *Zygote In My Coffee* (print and online) , and *Word Riot,* among others. Kaveh has never had his poems translated into another language, though a couple weeks ago he paid a British guy $5 to read one out loud.

Graffiti
(previously published in *Poesy*)

The clocks blink midnight as
you imagine scorching the room
with color. A Polaroid shows
a faded brick wall while another burns
into glorious Technicolor. Your
silhouette stands just out of frame,
a black outline melting into itself,
two hands dripping with
every color they've ever held,
a shape against the streetlights
moving to color the world with
something.

~Kaveh Akbar

hallelujah

(previously published in *remark*)

says she's been having a rough time
since her husband left.
she's been having money trouble.
says the sharks are at her throat.
says she's found Christ, been going to church.
says she's listening to AM, rooting Cubs, reading
Peanuts, staying sober, fucking straight no kinky stuff,
smoking less, reading the Bible, wearing
cotton, praying at night, drinking Kool-Aid.
smiles.
says she's got news, I won't believe it.
says she bought a lottery ticket.
played her birthday, won 20,000.
says Jesus heard her prayers.
says he's paying her back for all the bullshit.
says she's never been happier.

~Kaveh Akbar

ambidexterity

saw this guy on tv
who could write a
different verse of the bible
with his left hand, right hand,
left foot, and right foot
simultaneously.

i just sat there,
thinking about how
i can't even jack off
left-handed.

~Kaveh Akbar

William Taylor Jr.

For Any Of Us

The poems aren't faring very well today.

The sky looks tired
and newspaper headlines
tell of a girl with her head
chopped off.

I guess today's not too good
for any of us.

On the way to work I stop by a bar
and decide to stay there.

The people in the bar look the way people in bars
have always looked.
They talk too loud about the same things.

The same jokes are etched across the condom machines:

This gums tastes funny.

The same man sits in the same corner
and talks to someone I can't see.

I buy a beer for the girl with her head
chopped off
and we talk awhile until she gets bored
and says she has to go.

I ask if we can meet again and she says
she doesn't know.

I drink 4 more beers
and step outside

to find the sun has gone off sick
and the sky frightened with clouds
afraid to weep.
~William Taylor Jr.

Another Lie Handed Down Through the Ages Like a Phony Dollar Bill

Time never
healed much of anything.

Sometimes you look around

and all you see
are scars.

~William Taylor Jr.

Lovesong

The sun has burst
the moon's collapsed
the stars are busted
and the sky's a heavy blanket
of pitch
crumpled down
upon us
the ground's gone rotten
hollow
beneath our feet
the whole world broken
like some Christmas toy
of long ago
and we
we are that way too
stumbling towards oblivion
arm in arm
half-witted and ridiculous
drunk as god
laughing
into the darkness.

~William Taylor Jr.

Todd Moore

Todd Moore, the author of more than one hundred chapbooks and books, is one of the founders of the Outlaw Poetry movement. He is known for his long poem Dillinger. Those sections which have been published have been compared to the work of John Steinbeck and Cormac McCarthy. He is currently at work on a novel about Billy the Kid. Both he and his son Theron co-edit the online zine St. Vitus.

Todd's "is ringo" appeared in the chapbook BLOOD ON BLOOD, St. Vitus Press. "i was" and "the way" appeared in the British zine Rising.

i was

standing on the
railroad tracks
overpass &
the cop was
staring at
me from the
pavement
below leaning
against his
parked cruiser
arms folded
there was
no way for
him to make
it over the
tornado fence
& up the
steep embank
ment so he
just stared &
every once
in awhile
ran the
palm of
his hand
across his
holstered
pistol butt
finally i
gave him
my best
fuck you
smile &
flipped him
off

~todd moore   33

the way

i write
is strictly
fuck you
no cap
ital letters
no punc
tuation
the words
jammed
together
or all
smashed
up like bro
ken glass
crushed
pop cans
& used
condoms
the sen
tence is
either a
stutter
or a
scream
& i'm
waiting
to watch
it explode

~todd moore

is ringo

yr real name
i asked
he put his
right hand
thru a thick
carpet of
black hair
& sd you
want that
knife you
can have
it the switch
blade was
out on the
table & i
clicked it
shut i saw
the name in
a book &
then it was
mine you
ever feel
like you
were lost
ringo sd
nobody is
ever lost
in america
i sd ringo
sucked th
last of the
smoke out
of his cig
aret & sd
everybody
is lost in
america

~todd moore   *35*

P. H. Madore

P. H. Madore has been called a "firebrand" by lots of people who figure he should have been an abortion. Rumor has it that he doesn't trust your or any government. E-mail: phmadore@riseup.net;
support: http://litdispatch.net.

& You Fade Loudly Into The Past

Today's a windy January
& on the breeze I swear
I smell the bloodsalt of the future

Smuggling ideas in memories
Backpacks, burnworthy black flags
& cryptic symbols
 We appear to serve
 In aprons, hardhats, cheaper suits
 Smiles & record time

We're still around, apparently waiting
 Though should a child
 Stand in a breadline
 For a month then she'll grow
 & as such we have--
  smarter, stronger, & serious

Impossible's as much a loaded word
 As democratic rule & war on terror
 Are callow farces

We accept these no longer
 & pity you to doubt us
 Much more

You dine on platinum dishes
 Drug our children to sleepy submission
 Expect them to fight your monied wars
 Know not want, have never known need
 Lie to each other & to we inferiors

But I, a common sailor's son
Born a Yankee with no inheritance save that
Very birthstone of the first American revolution

I have no intention to lie to you:

    When our world is the world
    & you are openly reviled--
    When life is to be lived
    & you fade loudly into the past--
    When my brothers fear you no more
    & your whips prove dysfunctional--

On that particular hour
Fair quarter I'll give to cowards
& take none from swine will I
Because I died with each weekly
Rationing of my slave salary

& I cannot wait
To watch you halflings
Swing in the whirlwinds
By battered voiceless necks
Amongst the tortured echoes of your guilt

~ P. H. Madore

Cancel Their Apocalypse

"We sell ourselves every day." --Rise Against

Every morning I wake up repackaged
With thoughts, memories of all that led me here
Wondering if I was ever better off
Or if I ever will be
& my burning cigarette means weakness

I should just stand atop a roof & shout my lungs coarse:
"Mobilize! Not one more word 'till there's something to talk
about & moreover to look forward to! Throw a party on a
graveyard of police cars! Settle all scores & cancel their
apocalypse! Move into the White House! Revolt! Take what's
yours! Burn the liquor store, the lottery, the pawn shop, & the
bar! Fight these white-shirted sissies! Do not doubt yourselves!
Hold on for paradise goddammit!"

Every morning I wake up a bit more dead
Than the grinded day before
With wants, needs I may never fulfill
Wondering if I was ever better off
Or if I ever will be
& my drying pen means weakness.

~ P. H. Madore

Into An Upscale Café

Again homeless
Not hopeless

Could've had a bed
With a college sexpot overnight
But didn't seize the moment

Needed rest after much
Wandering with stranger who
Wrecked the moment with his sell-out laughter

Slept in a subway tunnel
& outside the station on the ground
To be awakened by some owner
& then stumbled into an upscale cafe

Where despots & racist professionals
Are served by immigrants who
Let me sleep another two hours
After which I caught up on
Your contemporary news

~ P. H. Madore

Katharine Polenberg

Katharine Polenberg's poems have appeared online in *Laura Hird's Showcase, Triptych Quarterly Fiction, Zygote in My Coffee, Thieves Jargon* and *Poor Mojo's Almanac(k)*, and forthcoming in *Cherry Bleeds*. She resembles a real person, living or dead. You can find more by visiting her at http://www.freewebs.com/outsiderartist/index.htm.

Discounted

There is this life
we open our lips
to cause this
starved meagerness
the paucity of the design
already apparent

at the birth and
there is this

pantomime of sterile
and baffled gestures with
shovels full of turned earth
marked by granite

a desperate quality to laughter
and smacks on the back telling
us we will take this death
we have already

~Katharine Polenberg

Jaw Breakers

candy & wallpaper were both ugly then
but childhood
had fluoride smiles
and red white and striped
foil and felt with bald spots in
the nicotine yellow
a stink of pink color mixed
with grays anatomy blues
it was washable

coated paper stamped with bugs
wings as big as bed sheets
frolicking quietly
off the under lying horsehair
plaster warped and peeling
landing in the mouths of children
like us so young

we had canines but
wisdoms didn't come
in for years no bite yet a dump
clean enough to stuff
with calico and swallow
some homespun filth
our jaws still elastic
enough to snap back fast
in shape for the
rote recital quote:

Fine, Thank you

~Katharine Polenberg

How do YOU do?

I tried
to elbow my way
into day
slow and polite
even slightly stooped
yet my head and hair
slam against
the displaced air
with the clanging impact
of a wrecking ball
hitting concrete

I tried
to apply the morning
to my skin
in careful titration
with a Q-tip
and still
it's raising welts

I tried
getting some coffee
in me but it dribbled
down my chin
my jaw shaking with the
mouthful of
jackhammer
I can't spit out

front teeth cutting
my " . . . effing?!" bottom lip
hot brown drops
cracking and chipping
my sternum

I know my heart
will break next over breakfast
as I ask myself-

what was it that got to you?

~Katharine Polenberg   44

J. D. Nelson

J. D. Nelson (b. 1971) experiments with words and sound in his subterranean laboratory. His poems have appeared in many small press publications, both print and online. J. D. lives in Colorado, USA. Visit www.MadVerse.com for more information.

bloodlord

chain gang
chain smoke
chain the bad dog

scrape my sins
from my skin

examine the rotten
inner workings
of our subterranean
filth maze

cleanse my eyes
with iodine

~J. D. Nelson

Originally published: *StrangeRoad* Sept. 2005

a spider's prayer

I hope my legs
aren't ripped off
one

by one.

~J. D. Nelson

Originally published: *Mad Swirl* Jan. 2007

stone face, tongue of dust

I've memorized
the contents of
this fun little dungeon

day follows day
my eyes follow
my body's shadow
across the walls

I'm in suspense,
wondering when
the rats will arrive.

~J. D. Nelson

Originally published: *Unlikely Stories* Feb. 2002

Sean Lyman Frasier

Sean Lyman Frasier is a screenwriter, film-maker, and poet who resides in New York City. He has won the Ithaca College Senior Screenwriting Award and several awards for his volumes of poetry. His volumes include "Dry Highways and Dead Boys," "A Coltish Lap-Stain Called America," and "Jelly Rat Orgy Tonight!" He is the creator of the website "Halving A Baby" and hopes to someday own a grey cat and name it Vladimir.

THE BEST DEFENSE

I have a brand new watch
and a woman I pay
to clean the extra rooms
in my home.
All day I dream
of human bones.

If you soak my hands
in boiling water
for two centuries
you wouldn't wash
the dark blood
out of my skin.

Stack my victims
and watch in awe
as the bloody edifice forms.
The tower of the dead
blocks the sun
and I smile.

The judge nods
and admires my suit.
After the trial is over
he asks where I had it tailored.
I give him a name and number
and he thanks me.

I run over a vagrant
on my way home from court.
His blood gleams on the asphalt.
I have my best defense
tucked in the shadows
of my bill fold.

If you wake up
screaming
into the blackness
there's a good chance
you were dreaming
of me.

~ *Sean Lyman Frasier*

THE LION MAN OF HUNTINGTON

There's another person missing in Huntington.
That makes six in one month.
If you ask anyone in the town
they'll tell you it's the Lion Man's doing.
From my perch in the tree
outside of Laurie Farmer's window
I watch the Lion Man drive down Main Street,
just like he always does at 5 A.M.,
delivering the Huntington Free Press.
The Lion Man has a head of thick greying hair
that surrounds his entire face like a mane
and he has small teeth that all come to a point.
The sharp teeth make him say, "Free Preth."
He has a pet lion named Ginger
that sleeps all day in the back of his station wagon.
Chief Trumble refuses to provide
any investigative information
but did release a statement
that the police force had two unnamed suspects,
one man and one lion.
There have been rumors
that the Lion Man eats the bodies,
or feeds them to Ginger,
or they eat the bodies together like lovers,
or he grinds the bones into fuel for his station wagon.
No one sits next to the Lion Man
at Chubby's Sports Bar anymore.
A week ago from my perch I saw Mr. Farmer
digging holes in his back yard during the small hours,
and while I was just passing Mayor Graham's window
a little after midnight
I saw him with his mistress, both naked,
admiring something in his closet.
The hardwood floors were slick with red.
Then there's Chief Trumble,

whose wife was the first to disappear.
I saw the Chief tiptoe down Main Street
with dark stains on his clothes
and something shiny in his hand
when I was resting behind a shrub
in the Hairston family's yard.
But if you ask anyone in this town,
there are six people missing in August,
and it's the Lion Man's doing.
At a town meeting Mr. Farmer said,
"We gotta find the monster who done all this."
As he spoke his fingers trembled
and I saw the purple shovel blisters on his hand,
the black dirt under his fingernails.
The Lion Man's station wagon rumbles down the street.
Ginger yawns and closes her eyes.
I turn back to Laurie's window
and watch her sleep.

~ Sean Lyman Frasier

When the Dead Walk Freely

When the other prisoners used to ask
if he really stabbed the woman ten times,
my great-grandfather shook his head
and said, "No. Never even met her."

Twelve years later,
his answer depended on his mood.

If he was bored and wanted to tell a story
he would say that the harlot had it coming,
or he would say he loved her more than God
and that some sonuvabitch framed him.

"True you stabbed her ten times, Frasier?"
"Nah. Must have been more like sixteen."

But when he wrote to his parents in Scotland,
or his children and wife in the Adirondacks
he would tell them that the woman he never knew
came to him every night in his cell.

"I tell her I'm sorry that her murderer
still walks and breathes freely," he wrote.

She came to him in many forms:
A woman with a blood-spattered veil and gown,
a skeleton weeping beneath his bunk,
a smiling beauty dressed in sunlight.

A month away from his fourteenth year
he was released when the killer confessed.

One of his final diary entries, eleven years after release:
"I dream more about her than I do my wife.
There can't be any true rest for the dead,
not when they walk in my dreams like so."

~ Sean Lyman Frasier

Kristin Bird

Kristin Bird's poems have appeared in *She-Stuff Magazine*.

Today I Am Not Such A Hero As Yesterday

I do not remember the fish tank blinking
above the couch in the living room.

It was surely lighted because of the hour.
I do not remember the material
of the blanket. I don't remember the hour.

I do not remember daybreak.
Neither of us were crazy,

no crazier than the other
or anyone else. I only remember relief
that needed no convincing.

The fish (Faulkner's fish, the small kind,
disinterested, named) was almost as huge
as ourselves.

I am amazed by all I do not remember.
We are pulled through the eye of the fish,
one tragedy after another.

~Kristin Bird

Do Not Worry That I Am Late

Do not worry that I am late,
dear, because I have stopped
in the cafe along the way
to your apartment.
Do not worry if I am late.
I am there, talking to,
or being talked to
by, a Polish man
who owns the place.

We are not in Poland.
People in coffee shops
like to talk,
and Europeans, especially,
love to talk. This time,
he had held a Russian stage,
black curtains on tan wood --
this, if you don't know
the color of wood, and curtains,
and Russians:

red, black and white, a star
on the actor's temple or the center
of his neck. Either way.
Europeans *in coffee shops,*
you'll find,
love to talk more than anyone,
because they have time.
They have all the time in the world.

~Kristin Bird

The Importance of Building Your Own Bomb Shelter

There is an economy,
not of spirit, but of balance,
in pictures of your mom and dad:

Banana split hair, a whale of a cigar.
Colors that didn't know any better.
The godforsaken carpet.

They saved lawns
one by one that year,
pretended time could be bought
with iron.

When morning came,
they were alone
and ecstatic:

Nobody but us, they said,
could be responsible for this.

They were thinking of the first
war, cat, cold.
The beautiful baby. The animal car.

~Kristin Bird

D. B. Cox

DB Cox is a blues musician/writer from South Carolina. His writing has been published in *Zygote In My Coffee, Remark, Underground Voices, Thunder Sandwich, Dublin Quarterly, Aesthetica, Bonfire, Gator Springs Gazette, Heat City Review, My Favorite Bullet* and *Open Wide Magazine.*

He has had three books published: *Passing For Blue* (published by RankStranger Press), *Lowdown* and *Ordinary Sorrows* (published by PuddingHouse Publications).

irretrievable things

small town
hallelujah hustler
hiding
behind stained-glass panes
throwing
a long shadow
over christ-faced
patrons
flim-flammed
congregation
fooled by
an empty scarecrow
concealing
dark places
behind
counterfeit eyes
tinted with
tiny blood-red
sketches
forever etched
against
the black canvas
of a twisted mind
ticking time—truth
gets lost
imaginary monsters
pay the cost
while
yellow ribbons
of old police tape
rot in the rain
of arkansas killing fields
and three

west Memphis
stand-ins
rust
in the belly
of a heavy
metal machine
and dream
of irretrievable things
~D.B. Cox

madly backwards

sirens sing
junkies to sleep
on the stairway
of the sunset hotel
old hopes fade
& dance away
madly backwards
rain reclaims
worn tire tracks
of piss-yellow cabs
pointed cross town
by gypsy hacks—
insomniacs from new york,
new jersey, new delhi
chasing american dreams
down empty streets—
red, white & blue illusions
slipping into the darkness
of rearview mirrors
lost in the shadows
of sacred skyscrapers
that sigh & bend
in the wind
old myths fade
& dance away
madly backwards

~D.B. Cox

repetition of a song

take me
to a place
where midnight
accumulates
don't want
to see the sun
anymore—put me
on a train
with no windows
where nighttime
lasts forever
& a speed-mad
engineer with
a mechanical heart
high balls
a coal-black engine
through
time tunnels
like a bullet
leaving a gun
where the speed
of darkness
is faster than
the speed of light
dreaming up
a nocturnal scene
mingus & monk softly
behind
a tan-skinned lady
white flower
in her hair
singing "keeps on a rainin'"
just give me things
i can depend on
red wine, old times
the repetition of a song

~D.B. Cox

Doug Draime

Doug Draime's most recent book is "Spiders And Madmen" (Scintillating Publications, 2006). He began publishing in the 'underground' and small press in the late 1960's, while living in Los Angeles, becoming part of the notorious L.A. poetry scene of the latter 20th Century. His writing (poetry, short stories and plays) continues to appear in magazines, newspapers, and online journals worldwide. He lives in the southern foothills of the Siskiyou range in Oregon.

"City Of the Dead" first appeared in *Blowback Magazine*
"Spiders And Madmen" first appeared in the *American Dissident* and is the title poem of my newest chapbook
"Lawyer For The Machine" first appeared in *Universal Poems Journal* (UN)

City Of The Dead

Black bodies floating like rotting
buoys through the former Mardi Gras streets.
Too bad no oil in the veins of the poor,
their ancestors slaves of the
republic: exploited, expendable,
expired through toxic, disease ridden waters.

Voodoo mind set of elected officials
stick pins through the hearts of common sense
and compassion, as they point their well-fed fingers
at each other, behind the glaring wall of their lies.

Bush, Cheney and Rumsfeld, their arrogance
and disrespect toward the lives of the dead, appalling!
These gross monsters of prevarication.
Three monkey politicians sitting in a row: hear no truth,
see no truth, speak no truth.
Black woman Rice without a hitch in her voice, without
a blink in her eye, without a trace of candor, saying
the shamefully hesitant response to the
catastrophic disaster not racially motivated.
May her ancestors raise up and bitch slap her, may the
bodies of the dead in New Orleans, raise up and
haunt the halls of her plush affluence, screaming her name:
Condeleeza, Condeleeza, Condeleeza.

~Doug Draime

Spiders And Madmen

Madmen hold their
greasy fingers
on the buttons,
while pigeons shit and
congregate
in Pershing Square.
As the fly is devoured by the
spider in the corner
of your living room;
its huge web a maze of
fly corpses.
Madmen trade your name
to other madmen.
You are nothing but a series of
numbers to them.
Or a piece of meat
meant for the butcher block.
Madmen think you are
nothing but a body to be
bought, then destroyed in mass
in the middle of a bright
full moon night.
Madmen see you as profit
or loss broadcast on CNN.
They don't care about your
immortal soul, and curse
you and your descendants behind
armored doors.
While pigeons still shit and
congregate in Pershing Square,
as thousands of fly corpses
fall down from the web in your living room,
blocking your frantic escape.

~Doug Draime

Lawyer For The Machine

brain child
of the dumb

ignorant by choice

wealthy
by theft

purely corrupt
by inclination

lying
because he knows
nothing else

doomed
by moral & spiritual
boomerangs
which he denies
or thinks are cons
though, he's the con
the Judas
the back stabber

knowing
the truth
then betraying it
with a kiss
to its brutal
death

~Doug Draime

Bryon D. Howell

Bryon D. Howell is a poet currently residing in New Haven, Connecticut. He has been writing poetry for a great number of years. Recently, work of his has appeared in *poeticdiversity, Red River Review* and *The Quirk.*

LIFE AND A STALE BALL OF GUM

Gumballs -
a quarter for each.

Once your child
turns the cold metal dial,
the show begins.

Round and round
it goes,
descending down
the swirly metal track thingy -
making a loud

BANG

once it has reached its
destination
at the bottom.

What are we teaching
our kids?

The downward
spiral
of innocence?

Trading your
dreams
for a thirty second
merry-go-round
of stale bubble gum?

That everyones
one big wish
can be granted

at the sounding of
one pointless
gunshot?

That same
quarter
will buy your kid two
fake soups
when it's
sentenced to life
in prison
for trying to steal
someone else's
gumballs
because it thinks -
they're fresher.

Know that
gumball
is probably significantly
older
than the child
who'll be chewing it.

And as far as
the obsession for all things
descending
buy a notebook
for about
50 cents
endless possibilities
and a helluva
lot more
colorful

spiraling.

~Bryon D. Howell

MY ANTHEM

Today I despise
eagles.

They prey
on squirrels.

The first time I
fed a squirrel
by hand
without being bitten,
was the last
time
I put my hand
over my heart
to salute the
American flag.

I got tired
of sacrificing
unconditional love
for a prayer
on two

cruel wings.

~Bryon D. Howell

LIFE AS AN ENDIVE SALAD

I'm living in the homeless shelter,
but I'm not really,
homeless.

Frankly,
I'd never make it
as a homeless man
walking the streets of
New Haven, Connecticut.

It took me the better part
of a week
to figure out how to
correctly fasten my over-sized bed-sheet
to the green, plastic mattress
so it didn't slip
anymore.

For all those years I ruthlessly
tossed salads,
I've now got
one trying to lose
me -

like a stale crouton.

~Bryon D. Howell

Joshua Kilbourn

Josh Kilbourn lives in the San Francisco Bay area, but spends his time roaming the West Coast and South America. Currently he is working on a collection of prose.

Be a good animal, true to your animal instincts.

I may be dangerous.... but I'm not crazy. Senses dulled. Unaware of anything in the Pacific North West.... Too many days, with little money and no heart. Depressed like most small rural towns and as dirty as and as cantankerous as the sprawled Metropolis. I'm not crazy... Maybe a little.... Long abusive late nights, early mornings craving more.

Mornings, belly up as the sun touches my face. Clothes damp from cloudy nights in parks. Half awake, too lazy to find adequate cover in the cool drunken night. And now, lying in the sun. The slow moving grey clouds blanket the sun. I am cold and alone, under grey cloud cover.

Those (under the bridge) kids are getting to me. Frayed wiring, with little hope of repair. Spend enough time with them and you'll find leisure and despair who's hotheaded. Mostly you befriend the bipolar- schizophrenic in the torn tye-dye shirt and camouflage shorts who tells you empty stories. "My wife died in the World Trade Center attacks bro", or how his daughter was born with a bad heart. "She needs an operation bro, she's in the hospital right now waiting for a donor". These rehearsed stories resonate unaffected, flint-heartedly. Cocksure victims having little chance, overcoming their own bullshit. Dope-bitten and destitute.

Fatigue sets in like slow decay. Wary from all the ugliness hiding on dark stoops, on wet sidewalks, in cracks leading into lush green paths and worn bridges. Loathsomeness, shaped into miserable men, women and

trolls. Dangerous Trolls, with dangerous pasts.
Murder, rape and larcenous behavior, inside the belly
of the beast. Hordes of Trolls, holding up under
bridges and peeking through well maintained city
gardens. Ready to pounce.

Small towns with unmistakable lines running rapidly on
the power grid, North, South, East and West.
Inescapable, unremarkable.

The seemingly long and wearisome trip home. Well kept,
warmly wrapped in a blanket with skeptical-depression.
A probable recovery, left with superficial scars.

~Joshua Kilbourn

sing the sad songs

Mild distortion seeps slowly into suburban dwellings
of the well fed without notice. Awkward feelings on
windy nights in cities that always sleep. It's hard to
learn anything that had not been taught. These are the
days.

Simple days of well trimmed green lawns and well
placed outdoor ornaments. Old, tired mailmen walking
and not so vicious dogs barking, Drunk, miserable
husbands and fat, lying wives fighting. Sweet young
girls sneaking and deviant, bravado boys watching.
These are the days .

Uneventful days, fade colorlessly into long dark dull
nights. Anger grows in resistance from the looming
grey areas. Late nights of unwasted frustration. I can
not bare one more night with the snores and screeches
of the dull. Hopeless. The cleaning, the correcting,
the arguing, the loving, the fighting, the fucking,
the feeding, the laughing. These are the days.

My brain is a deep sea cavern, a treasure chest at
its core, filled with opiates and beer. Anecdotes to
slow the flow of apathy and disgust. Blurry eyed,
peering out from a window in this neon bar, drab cold
weather.

Today is a fight against the mundane ills of this
mortal coil. The life ordinaries' fists will beat you
down. Bloodshot visions of disorder resting atop
bus-stop-benches, building stoops, corners, walls and
windows...... plagued. Illness is everywhere.

These are the days of youth. Cherish it for it is
short lived. Cherish your hard-on for it is fleeting,
cherish fucking for it is fleeting. Cherish no life at
all, for it is worthless. Cherish your beatings as you
will remember them. Love can take you over and destroy
you with one fell swoop!

Fleeting pavement, fixed lights, fixed signs, rolling
darkness. Sweet depression comes in as a thick layer
of fog. Clouds line my now dark, deep sea cavern with
gloom, and mud. This thin shell of a head is a dark
and dirty place. A head full of mishap and
disillusions, lost and misplaced memories.

Northern winds howl over broken fences and rustling
overgrown weeds. Dogshit flanks my back yard. Drunk
and momentarily fearless, as I walk down streets named
after states. Eyes peer out of poorly lit windows.
wired blockheads, looming, fixing, repairing in
garages of feeble homes. Tired buildings and brown
horizons line the shadowed city at a boring pace.

~Joshua Kilbourn

Lucid assembling on the freedom line

Welcome to the land of the living, now pick up a
shovel and start digging. Start digging you cowards,
you faggots! You crying, niggardly maggots! Dig! Heave
and hoe!

Scammed, coerced and tricked into absurd scenarios, with
those who suffer selfishly. Firmly planted underneath
thumbs of Asshole's with large debts and fractured
aspiration. Walking the earth wielding heavy-chains
and bats.

Grim production lines: Conveyor belts running
continually..... Dawn turns to dusk. Daunting moments
in time with reoccurring nightmares, followed by false
promises.

Minotaurs: Well trained managers and supervisors, lure
ailing souls off and on the line. Scraped knuckles and
flaccid muscles. Breaking backs. Deep impressions of
soles on souls.

Quick breaks induce short lived dreams. Abstract
colors and surreal visions shimmer quickly with
comfort. Time descends into long passageways. Dark
corners pour into illuminating myths, submerged in
vivid resonance.... Lucid assembling on the freedom
line. Sudden glory, ruthful in sleep. Agony and spoil,
ruthful in wake.

Scattered Goods: A new term for shit... Piss, diapers
and dead-goldfish. Blistered on beaches..... boils on
skin. Ignorant without sin. A candid glimpse, an
unseemly look into the frivolous past, present and

future. Gaudy gestures rest heavy on weary silhouettes. Ominous statues and pungent fumes. Shades of illness and depravity color the horizon.

Rotten teeth are signs of good living under bad conditions. Sores, pustules and scars tatter the body. Signs of good living in hazardous times. Permanent reminders of necessary decay, a steady descent.

Revolving with fewer rotations. Last chance for a slow dance. Constricted blood vessels, wrapped tightly around strained, popping and narrow eyes. Nothing left to lose, when your riding the spiral with quick turns. Sudden stops are always a killer. Remorse, wanton lust and terrible regret, in the final moment before the abrupt drop off.

~Joshua Kilbourn

Victor Schwartzman

Victor Schwartzman was born and raised in Brooklyn, but moved to Canada when the government wanted him to kill people in Vietnam he never met. Looks like, with the West Memphis Three, the government is still at it. Now he lives in Canada, has a day job as a Human Rights Officer, and at night writes. He runs a book review blog at http://ulabookreview.blogspot.com, a personal blog at http://victorhypertension.blogspot.com, and you can find ten chapters of a graphic novel at http://victorschwartzman.tripod.com. He says: will it not be a great day when our governments stop killing people?

Pornography, Nazis and the Internet

When the Nazis came to power
they outlawed pornography:
it is difficult to plan conquering the world
while you are jerking off.
But after they invaded a country
they spread pornography there
it is hard to fight your oppressor
if you are busy stroking yourself.

Now, look at the internet today.
Pornography has spread everywhere.
We were invaded years ago
but were too busy pleasuring ourselves
to notice or to ask,
who are today's Nazis?

~Victor Schwartzman

How Many Ways Do You and I Masturbate?

How many ways do you and I masturbate?
So many, I run out of fingers counting them:
brainstorming irrelevant ideas at a meeting
talking about giving the poor money
sending emails to friends when your short story is published
looking into the mirror as you try comb-overs
reading Joyce when someone else is looking
taking dates to movies with subtitles
rooting for the team that is winning
telling parents about that possible promotion
owning an SUV
wearing the latest fashions
attending the best parties
going to the gym to sculpt your body

See? I'm starting to run out of toes now.
writing a poem

~Victor Schwartzman

What If I Had Only A Few Hours To Live?

At any time I could walk outside and be hit by a falling space
toilet.
So. Should I:
pay these bills--so I won't leave debts?
watch tv--and laugh my hours away?
do the laundry--so my corpse will be freshly dressed?
take a nap--so I die refreshed?
mow the lawn--so the neighbors will feel better?
ground my daughter--for staying out late and enjoying life?
say good-bye to my family--or try to take them with me?
make love or have sex--can I do both at the same time?
go for a walk--so I will croak physically fit?

What if I had only a few hours to live?
Maybe I need more time.

~Victor Schwartzman

April-May March

April-May March is a Factory Girl from Norwich, England.

Stay Silent

I can't remember that much
but I can see the dust and trees.
The radio plays Shirley Brown
as days pass without meaning

The fields in which we used to play
stay silent in hot summer.

Fixate on the grey
its on the walls
and in the clouds.
Pass the hours away by the river
in the time you are allowed

~April-May March

Contralto

I got a ravishing hunger
that provokes dank movement
creaking on steps
ready to burst

the rickety woodworm invested stair rail
guides me through the blinding darkness.
I discover sunlight
on the verge on disintegration

~April-May March

Time don't matter

Here I sit in my cage
with no regrets
for I have done nothing wrong.

Circumstances conspire against me
the wind blew me down.
I sit in isolation
wishing for a hand to hold

Time don't matter
i've got bags of it
to ponder all kinds of shit

people I will never meet
places I will never see
time don't matter

~April-May March

Matt Finney

Matt Finney is a white trash poet who burns his ass up in a small Alabama town.

Roll Tide

His oil covered hands
Left black stains on the
Sweating Miller bottle
He handed it to me
While momma was
Out of the room
Letting my 6 year old fingers
Grip it and take my first
(But not last)
Sip
I sat on the couch
And he threw his hat at the
Seat next to me
This was my first time watching
A football game
Alabama V. Auburn
And my dad was never one for hope
But he wanted his boy to grow up
A Roll Tide fan
And for the first time
In a real long time
Hope filled him up
And Auburn fumbled.

~Matt Finney

Putting Up a Bulldog Front

I'm out here
In the backyard burning up
Thinking of nothing
With the stereo blaring
13 Songs
By Fugazi
They've shut up the whole goddamn neighborhood
And while I don't agree with their views on
Beer and shit
They got a screaming motherfucker
And that's all that counts right about now.

~Matt Finney

Disintegration of Three

The "Satanic Panic"
Made them run for their
Leather bound Bibles
Kicked morals back in gear
And caused a bounty back on
Black t-shirts
I hate to say it
But God's turned the other cheek
It's ok though
Y'all got Robert Smith on your side
And judging by past performances
He's the only one you'll need.

~Matt Finney

Michael D. Grover

Michael D. Grover is a Florida born poet. In the late 90's he moved to Los Angeles where he really found his poetic voice. He found a poetic movement in Larry Jaffe's Poetic License. There he learned most of what he knows about poetry and performance.

From there Michael moved to Philadelphia, where he and another poet Natalie C. Felix started the poetry series Uni-Verse-All Voices which started at the world famous Five Spot, and ended two years later at The Friends Meeting House.

Michael has featured and read his poetry all over the country. Michael's poetry has been published all over the world, including in print Citizen 32, Alphabeat Soup, The San Gabriel Poetry Quarterly, Mad Poets Review, Philadelphia Poets and the anthology One Drop: To Be The Color Black, and online including www.getunderground.com, www.kissthebeat.com, and www.dyingwriters.com , and the October issue of DecomP Literary Magazine.

Michael is now back in Florida from there he hosts the website www.covertpoetics.com, and hosts a monthly reading at Exodus Coffee & Culture in Port Saint Lucie.

Ars Poetica #6

Poetry doesn't care who has the highest score,
The fanciest clothes, the coolest lines
Or who's got the cool Hardy Boy's hand gestures,
Poetry would turn on the TV for basic entertainment.
Poetry does not want fame or fortune.
Poetry just wants respect.

When I was living in LA
I had to take the Metro,
Sometimes instead of those
Ads on top of the window
They would have Poems there.
That's what Poetry wants,
A ride on the bus.
Right there with the people
To be read by the poor and common folks
On the way to or from their miserable jobs.
Poetry likes riding on the bus.
Poetry thinks it should ride on the bus more often.

But all too often it's read in stuffy institutions
By stuffy people, in stuffy suits
Reading stuffy pseudo Poetry.
Let the real thing flow baby!

Let Poetry run wild in the streets
And possess the hearts of the dispossessed
Give them something to believe in,
Give them Poetry.

Sean Sannemin told me himself
In Maurice's front yard on a clear night in Glendale
(Every night's a clear night in Glendale.)
"Go with your Poetry, nothing will make you freer."

Since that very moment I have lived my life
To spread that message that Sean spread to me.
He bestowed on me this awesome responsibility.
To testify the word of Poetry!
And I won't back down!

Poetry it liberates
        It animates
        Rejuvenates!

Poetry rocks,
It rolls,
It hip-hops over my soul.
Keeps me sane in an insane world.

Poetry is my soul,
        My religion,
My deepest darkest secrets on a page,
And I'm not scared anymore.

Poetry is my flag,
My sovereign nation
And I will defend it
Until the day I die.

Poetry wants to be spread to the people.
Poetry wants to liberate the people.
The storm clouds are on the horizon,
The time is coming.
Set the mother fucker free!

~Michael D. Grover
(Originally published in the San Gabriel Poetry Quarterly)

Three Year Old Adidas

My Adidas are three years old - Saul Williams

Veteran of this class war
I wait.
Knowing the law of impermanence.
All that is permanent.
This aint gonna last.
This could never last.

I ask myself if things ever got this bad.
My Adidas really are three years old.
This aint no hip hop fantasy.
This is all american reality.
Artist I have always struggled.
I always got by.

Truth is I have always been too free
To be tied down to country.
But this is where I was born.
This is where I live.
This is where I break a sweat as I write this.
It's been too long now.

Total state of confusion
Where everything you look at seems like an illusion.
No, Neo is not coming to save us.
President and Governor bush are gonna kill us with kindness.

My friend keeps asking me
How we are going to get rich.
Do I look like a man
That's gonna get rich anytime soon?
Do I look like a man
That cares?

The fact is I don't bow to corporate religions,
Or any other kind of rotten system.
Greased in the blood of slaves.
Greased in dollars and cents.
I was trying to explain to someone in class today
How that was not a real american flag
Because of the golden tassels.
He didn't get it.
I didn't expect him to.

You can call me a dreamer
Because I'd rather live in a world free of suffering.
Free of the anxiety of
Big Brother constantly watching.
Free of the violence of poverty.
Free of the violence of war overseas.
Free of the violence of fifty bullets through the windshield.
Free of the hypocrisy of governments
That say they were elected,
That say they serve the people.

*~**Michael D. Grover***
(Originally Published in Citizen 32)

Dead Letter Room

There's a dead letter room.
For love letters never sent.
No need for stamps in there.
The just sit collecting dust
Full of missed opportunities,
And love unrequited.

There's a dead letter room.
A separate room
For all the love gone bad letters never sent.
It has to be twice as tall and wide.
A few letters in the other room,
Many letters in this room with my name on them.

Baby, when I look at you I see
Beauty grace and Poetry.
Baby, when I look at you I see
Those damn letters piling up again.
When I look at you I feel butterflies fluttering
Into nets, put in jars, so they don't fly around anymore.
All this beauty!
All this tragedy!

If love does have a fairy tale ending
It was poorly written.
If love is an act of faith,
I sink when I step onto the water.
If the dues must be paid,
I'm still waiting for the check.
This place was overpriced anyway.
Not even fast food comes cheap anymore.

Another soon to be dysfunctional love story.
More fodder for Jerry Springer.
Talk show america is hungry.
So baby let's get the show over with.
   ~Michael D. Grover   97

Jacob McArthur Mooney

Jacob McArthur Mooney lives in Canada where he works very hard to support his education habit and plays very hard to support his poetry habit. He believes in justice for the innocent and mercy for the guilty.

A Guide to Disempowerment

A woman in this building
lived with her two young
kids on the federal cheques. She cleaned houses to
buy extras, one of her
clients was the wife of a local
government official. When he found out, he called
his boss, then the lady lost
the welfare, then
her car, then
the kids. A sad story. A real
sad story. Unsure who

to dedicate the poem to; skinny children don't eat
ink and paper, and the client's husband never
told her what happened, they vowed
to keep work and family
life separate. The only thing left
                                   (well, in fact there's
nothing left, but a moralist hangs his
hat on what he finds—)
                       is the
government official. This poem is dedicated
to his valued honesty, his sense of
good works, the institution that granted
his professional degree
                       (…his bedroom community, Jean-
Jacques
              Rousseau, the founders of the nation...)

~ Jacob McArthur Mooney

A Guide to Remaining Skeptical about your Power as a Voter

Market Value= two men walking
down a rocky path holding a paved
road over their heads. One turns to
the other and as the concrete crumbles

around their bleeding hands, he says
This revolution is all spin, you know.
The revolution is all spin. A woman
stares until she sees a pack of cross-eyed

faces in the pattern of her wallpaper.
As she drifts outstretched to meet them,
she feels their focus resettling on
her face, but when she gets too close they (regrettably)

reset to looking nowhere. Once the
woman hits the wall cold against her
forehead, her hazel eyes neutral off.
She leaves a note on the noteboard, *The revolution*

is all spin. The revolution is all spin. Every-
thing the world needs to know about you
fits in most-used pockets of your purse.
Don't be angry or surprised. The revolution,

the revolution, the revolution is all spin. So
give me your vengeful dancing, your
daylong intellectual riffs. Give me
a taste of that hot wax, burning. Give

me the revolution, the revolution is all
spin. The revolution (devolution) the
revolution is all spin.
~ *Jacob McArthur Mooney*

A Guide to Punishment

Alright. So now here's one for the martyrs among us. Everyone
in this poem wears a uniform, *sowatchout.*

You pay for attention with your tax dollars, citizens, the whole
value of revenge
is the first three seconds post-impact. If you miss it there's no
encore.
They can build it up with better lighting, or a strong
performance
from the vanquished.

What we need is to be told that we're disgusting. What we get
is a reminder
of the bluntness of our organs, their tendency to leak when
attacked.

Moses took dictation to the best of his talents, but it's hard to
write on rock and
and he missed the amendment about the rules
only counting once per head. It's okay if the names run
together
or are hard to pronounce, faces are either covered or (in the
name of the humane)
strapped-back so The Gallery can't see them.

If I knew an elected official, I'd recommend
that the families be
seated in the same room. If the point is to transplant suffering,
imagine
how looking in the son-of-a-bitch's mother's eyes would
add value to the acquisition. There's votes there for an
innovator.

Saying it almost never happens is like saying it never happened to you.
Any argument based on statistics just
paints the room a darker red. Choose your conclusion: either a shade approaching black

$$\text{or}$$
$$\text{one that}$$
mixes uniform in blood.

~Jacob McArthur Mooney

Rob Plath

Rob Plath is 37 years old. He's from New York. He has one book of published poems called *Ashtrays and Bulls* (2003 1st place winner of *Nerve Cowboy*'s chapbook contest). He has published a lot of poems in journals and magazines: Barfing Dog Press, Big City Lit, Blowback, Cerebral Catalyst, Chiron Review, Devil Blossoms, Gnome, Long Islander, Long Island Quarterly, Lunatic Chameleon, Mad Swirl, Mannequin Envy, Nerve Cowboy, Pearl, Poetrybay, Polarity, Sho, Showcase Press Poetry Journal, Soul Fountain, Stickman Review, Strange Road, The Idiot, and Zygote in my Coffee. He has poems forthcoming in decomP, Mastodon Dentist, Laura Hird's Showcase, Dying Writers, ragged Edge , Winamop, Nerve Cowboy, Underground Voices, and Zygote in my Coffee (print).

In 2002, he was part of a spoken word/music CD "Northport Celebrates Jack" (a Kerouac tribute) featuring world famous musician David Amram. He was also a student of Allen Ginsberg's for two years.

poetry

is smoking
two cigarettes
at once
while passing
a fucking hearse
at 90+
in your
shimmying
old
compact car

~Rob Plath

right now you hold the aces

when you die someone will wear your pants, maybe your shoes

someone will feel up your woman, maybe fuck her better than
you did
maybe even eat her box when she's on the rag

when you die someone will keep their dirty buttplugs in your
dresser drawer
where you kept your clean socks

some coward will slap the shit out of your daughter, bruise her
cheek

when you die someone will buy a book with your leftover
money, one
you would've fucking despised, maybe one with raised lettering
on the cover

someone will sit in your chair and fart out the gasses of foods
you would've detested

when you die someone will dump all your poems, magazines,
journals into the fire

but for now, for right now, they all fold their hands down in
front of you

for now, you hold the fucking aces

~Rob Plath

like a mole ripped from its dark tunnel

i moved in with my woman
after much convincing from her
to let go of my subterranean pit
i've hidden in for the past 6 years
it had thick glass block windows
and dark wooden walls
and ontop of that i kept wool blankets
over the few windows to keep
the motherfucking sun out
it was a grave beneath a grave
and now i'm above ground
with lots of windows
lots and lots of windows
sometimes i feel watched
sometimes i feel itchy from sunbeams
sometimes i feel like a fighting fish placed
in a tiny bowl along with another
fighting fish
with a big cat's fang-face mooning over
the lip of the fucking bowl
doom coming at me from inside
and outside, everywhere

~Rob Plath

Pat King

Pat King, 26, spent a good portion of his life in Alabama and somehow wound up in Parts Unknown, Maryland. He digs Sylvia Plath and William Burroughs. He's a long standing member of the Underground Literary Alliance and currently runs their creative writing blog (www.undergroundliteraryalliance.blogspot.com). Pat is the fiction and poetry editor for outsiderwriters.org. Contact him at Alabamamoviemaker@hotmail.com.

A Clock

A person who exists in two
Times at once
A person two times once
A sonic regulation

A person who becomes a man of his
Own time becomes a clock becomes
A regulatory commission

A person's regulatory commission turns
Its back on personal time becomes free
To pursue time (a beach house)

A person of sonic regulation whose memory reminds him
Of something beyond the regulatory body
Legislating time reminds a sonic pastor of his own time
becomes

A man that exists in two times at any time considers the mode
of time
the greedy trick of time and time again I remind you need I
remind you
of time?

~Pat King

A Clock Tower

Had Debbie more than three lives to give for her mistress?
Lisa
"MOVIE"
Starr

Lisa MOVIE Starr born on the moon
In the summer of Poe
Lisa, caught between a nervous throat
And the exclusive TV rights to movie
Of her life of the week.

Religious rite of the show (in progress, take yer seats)
Lisa MOVIE Starr selling bigwigs and ties and TV
Eating ice cream out of a cowboy's boot.

On stage, in an attic above a porno movie theater
Lisa needs Debbie because the two of them are
Education
Errr….
"Showtime Girls"
They sing soothing songs

"Don't forget to write when you're mad foaming Vegas stars."

But there was no one to sing to.

~Pat King

Clock Unwound

They say the South
Will rise again
It already has
Like reverse clockwork.

Bush is the king of America the King of the South and the
Southern order rides the angry horse
Through screaming villages
Burning
They reverse time because
It pulls a sweet dark blanket
Over a twisted spine

An imaginary cause
A cause because to celebrate
Is to begin to tear away from
The cause.

Because to begin in the basement,
The party full and full of joy
And to begin to drink
(Laughter, two lovers fucking)
Is a clock moving time forward
To twist the spine again
Into its proper place.

~Pat King

Laura Vladimirova

Laura Vladimirova was born in Kiev, Ukraine. Looking to escape religious persecution, her family gathered their rubles and headed to Brooklyn, NY, where Laura occasionally resides. She has been writing poetry since she first learned how to speak and write in English.

This Happened

This happened: pushed down, against the ground
without tongue to cry
for youth's lost grasp
and stood, behind walls
without cries of youth's lost choice

Punished with doubt
a haze of uncertainty to rise up
in the nights of the now men,
who cry for their lost youth.

~Laura Vladimirova

This might be the first sentence ever written

This might be the first sentence ever written
Is anything spelled right?

This might be something I make sense of:

I haven't had a milkshake
since I realized that you'll inevitably die one day
I was immediately heartbroken,
one day there will be no you.

For you,
I stored crosses in shoeboxes.
I was too sad to do anything else.

This stomach ache is eating me whole
and through all this,
the pigeons don't even knows it's rush hour.

~Laura Vladimirova

Been Slow

Somehow the placidity of this warm bed
and warm body
has managed to dull the duties of cold,
dirty soles.

Waiting still under bridges for
the car noise and the train noise
to take off, fly off
like a flock of migrating geese mid-September

something through the birch trees once whistled
the tune of motion,
but at the same time it seemed safer at home,
wherever that was.

This old, stale love has since severed limbs,
hacked them off in chunks with a polished letter opener

and now this inability to roam, because
the only way to really beat the cold—
even when it's freezing outside—is to run.

~Laura Vladimirova

Rachel Kaplan

Upon graduating from the University of Florida, Rachel Kaplan left the Sunshine State to tackle Torah at Pardes Institute. She returned to the States to intern at Elat Chayyim Jewish Retreat Center. When she's not raising funds for Kehilat Romemu (romemu.org) and awareness of integral spiritual Judaism, Rachel studies Yang style Taijiquan, Choy Ley Fut, & other disciplines that aid her in defending the forces of good against evil.

Unheard Ranting Lost in the Stutter...

Who are they to judge me?
I'm in the majority here; so I happen to find it a fate worse than
death.
I open my mouth to speak but fear soaks up my words before
they can escape.
And they fear me.
Who can trust a man who can't trust his own tongue?
It's a vicious cycle.

They stare past me to a time or place rich with flavor.
They see me as vanilla.
I know that upon this podium is effervescent simplicity,
Earnestness coming out my ears
They never really tried to understand me.
No one gives vanilla the attention it deserves.

If only my heart sprouted lips, I could teach them in a way they
could trust. But the line between my heart and mind is fuzzy at
best.

I envy the auctioneer.
That fast-talkin' son-of-a-gun could be raging against the tides
of time,
in addition to original Italian armoires.
But eloquence does not beget the earnest.
How do I make them see?

Perhaps in my next life I will be the man with the untie-able
tongue,
Center ring.
Till then, I'll reside in the freak show.
I cannot speak for all the freaks;
Some are content here.
I did not ask for the title. Society branded me.

It's always those that believe in the relevance of titles that bestow them upon the unredeemed.
If the title never existed in my personal history, they'd be forced to open the book.
Who are they to judge me?

It's the tired and the hungry that they can learn from.
It's the tales of the weak and the downtrodden that can inspire the masses. It's the unconditional love of one who met condition after condition across the board that is most cherished.
Those who make these tiresome rules will never win the game.
I pray they don't wait till my next life to lose the rulebook.
It's a vicious cycle.

~Rachel Kaplan

Moving Slowly

Moving slowly to capture every grimace,
Every smiling coming my way.
I am an observer, not a fly on the wall.
I am noticed and I take notice.
Always years before my time,
But all the time aware of my ever-present youth.
My age is catching up with me,
And ancient souls do not fight the unknown, the Now.
I move with it, slowly.
Slippery slopes, they build character.
Superfluous character unasked for, unwanted.
What then is needed?
Only love.
Simple. True. Undisturbed by grips or ground.
Letting go,
And flowing from smile to grimace to glowing lovely smile.
Little girl lost in the shuffle,
Scraping her knees on gravel too fine to grip.
She never tried to grow up to fast; she never wanted to at all.
Stay in Neverland: a plausible goal for those born young.
But for those born ancient, a regression.
Another path taken,
Etched and gripped and slid upon and fallen over and
sometimes followed,
Sometimes far behind footsteps planted.
Often skipped over completely.
Too often? Still too young to tell.
Lost little girl.
How could I lose my way?
The way is mine and mine alone.
Followed maybe, but not stolen.
Shifted drastically but never erased.

Elderly children do well in kindergarten.
Willing to share, wiling to be guided,
But not so perceptive in finding a guide.
Fires once burned once lighted my way.
Ashes still hot, I feel them on me, in me.
Ashes,
Buried or blowing through the wind.
Ashes still hot but growing cold, dim,
Fading into the desert sands of journeys past.
Maybe fires are not made but entered into.
Moving slowly,
Searching horizons for flames turned red, orange, blue, white,
And blue all over again.
And fuel to revive it all.
Moving ever so slowly.

~Rachel Kaplan

The Sun Some Don't See...

He asked me to hop a train to Madrid, just for the weekend.
It'd be a nice change of pace from the Andalucian sun. But I
like Sevillian sunsets, so I decided to see another sunrise.

Thursday, March 11th, 2004.

The largest terrorist attack Europe has seen. 191 lives were
lost that morning at the train station in Madrid.

And I had decided to see another sunrise.

Spain shut down, as did the heavens. Black ribbons and grey
skies enveloped *Sevilla, y todo de España.*

I walked through empty streets and abandoned plazas. As I
walked, I spoke, in English, with a friend about the events
that occurred on elevenths of various months, and if
elevenths would ever be free from sorrow, anguish, or fear.

An elderly gentleman approached. He took the hat from his
head and placed it atop his cane. Both of his eyes starred into
mine, both of our eyes welling up.

"Y ahora, yo lo sé," he said. "Now I know, I know how your
people feel."

My people. But now I live in your country.

Is this what it takes to see? Are we obliged to be up close
and personal on the verge of extinction to empathize?

I thought about the business people, the politicians,

The police officers, the firefighters,
The lawmakers, the lawbreakers
The teachers, the students,
The lovers, the mothers,
The comedians and humanitarians that lost their lives to elevenths.
The blood, sweat, and tears of these lives don't speak language. How many elevenths will drive to fear this life?

As the sun sets over Andalucia, I pray that I will see yet another sunrise, and I pray for those that never will.

~Rachel Kaplan

Paul Tristram

Paul Tristram's poems have appeared in Poetry Cornwall, Purple Patch, Phoenix New Life, Inclement, Decanto, Pulsar, The Ugly Tree, Reach, Poetry Monthly, Moodswing, The International Journal Of Erotica and In Between Hangovers. His chapbook *…always lost and lost always… .Poetry From The Street.* was recently published by Cat Scan Press.

The Snakes Of Desire

"Milk, reminds me of my cum."
she giggled, licking her fingers.
"Thanks for inviting me back.
I knew that it would be you,
as soon as I looked into your eyes.
I could tell that you were
a Dirty Bastard.
I just had to come out tonight,
I've been having the same dream
for a whole week.
I'm walking down a burgundy
tunnel, the walls are velvet
and trickling with moisture
which has an aroma of
musky perfume.
I don't say anything out loud
but inside my head
I keep repeating
'I'm looking for the Snakes of Desire.'
Then I wake up sweating.
It's very strange and very horny.
Anyway, come back on top of me
and let me clean your face
with my mouth."

~Paul Tristram

Time For Ripeness

She coughed and shuddered
then out it came,
slipping perfectly
like a lollipop
being sucked the wrong way.
It hovered for a moment
then started to float upwards,
she sat in awe
watching the embryo
turn to a baby
within the ever growing
floating teardrop
before her.
She reached out her hand
but the baby changed to a tree
and before the tree had acorned
she had awoken, sat up in bed
and began to weave daydreams
and childhood memories
into the silken smoke
of her first cigarette,
deciding finally
to no longer eat the pill.

~Paul Tristram

My Day's Coming

Her finger's scratching,
disregarding sentimentality,
unconsciously collecting
my DNA.
She likes this
irregular, spontaneous
copulation,
it makes her feel.
As much as I enjoy
fucking her
one day
I'll meet someone
and the feather hairs
will fold into place.
Still unsure,
yet fulfilled
equally.
Surely that will be enough?

~Paul Tristram

Colin Dardis

Originally from Omagh in Northern Ireland, Colin Dardis now resides in Belfast, where he currently hosts a monthly poetry night in the Safehouse Gallery, and is a member of the performance group The Belfast Poets.

Colin is also the editor of Speech Therapy, a small poetry journal focusing on new poetry from the North of Ireland.

Colin's work has been published in the Black Mountain Review, Poetry Now, Unquiet Desperation, Laika Poetry Review, Revival and In Between Hangovers, amongst others. He hopes to continue to support and promote the poetry scene in Belfast and beyond, and is working toward a first collection of his work.

Poverty is in the richness of man's soul

Poverty isn't
sleeping under blankets of ice,
eating candy bars for dinner
or staining innards
with piss cheap
table wine.
It isn't the creditors
at your door
or the wolves
who think they know hunger.
It's chilblained lips,
kitchen sink nails
and teabag eyes.
Poverty comes
when the phone doesn't ring,
not when you can't afford
to keep it ringing.
It's when no one blesses
your doorstep
instead of unopened bills
pushed past the mat
like dead leaves
swimming
in a winter gutter.
It's when the day
is so dark
that you can't afford
to light a candle
for your own heart
and no one wants
to lend you
their flame.

~Colin Dardis

Asleep, like how a corpse may dream

I tried reading
some Bukowski
but I just
wasn't feeling it
so I corpsed out
like a dead poet
in this funeral bed
of mine.
the night wind
pressing against
the rented window
like mourners
pacing down
a church isle.
the blood not reaching
my vital organs,
my tattered heart,
bruised liver,
my whither brain,
with eyes
on the verge of drowning
they were barrels
perched on top
of waterfalls.
I was cold
and wanted peace.
It came
in the form of sleep.
The morning came next
to rape me
of my dreams.

~*Colin Dardis*

Resolve

Previous promises
have been kind to me:

I have resolved
to take up smoking
to drink more gin
to gradually get worse
as the years get on.

All this striving to improve,
pointless resolutions
abandoned at the first
whiff of temptation:
the sudden invite for a night out,
the chocolate cake at the café counter,
the cold January winds
keeping us away from the gym.

We'll rather dissolve into our deathbeds
than resolve our lives.

~Colin Dardis

Paul Corman-Roberts

Paul Corman-Roberts is the author of "Coming
World Gone World (The Abomunauts Are Coming To Piss On
Your Lawn)." He lives in California.
(www.paulcormanroberts.com)

THE CLOSET WITHIN A CLOSET

low, flickering fluorescent holding back
the thick, goopy curfew.

I chew and gag
on the vice of a thousand kings before
   backing into a corner with the rat reflex

beating back roaches with the pine sol pistol
beating back roaches on their backs

squealing
free
to crawl down into the detergent jungle
the anti-bacterial realm deadly to all

hacks. Olly-olly oxen free in the antiseptic
apocalypse
   gaze burning through the clove nicotine atmosphere
   revelation a rising wisp of smoke from the drain

I want to be a cockroach
to break down like a god, a soul particle
join the minions' romp across the wasteland
  the boundless across

Alas, the crickets are a tuned in and beautiful people
   beyond the ways of my too deeply set species.

So we wade back out into the
   thick goopy curfew ink, we

crawl beneath the earmuff helmets
drown in radio waves
wishing in vain
that they will carry us
far

from our closet within a closet.

~*Paul Corman-Roberts*

DOWN AND OUT IN PETROLIA

Federal agents of the drug war
with the coming of daylight,

play the "I'm kinkier than you" masque
scaled up about 1,000 feet every day

And look at their realm puzzled.
"Why does it not obey the laws of God?"

(And look at their cities)

Other Indian legends in America
 tell of bear men
      wolf men
      tribes of the forest.

This could never happen at a 49'ers game.

The stranger was sensed as
Greatest menace
in ancient communities.

~Paul Corman-Roberts

WHITE FLIGHT IN TIME MACHINES

The consequence of what her sire had said
:All my memories are trapped in a heaven
the inner cylinder the unlikely
green heart of this ripe
Disney dream of Homecoming.
Certainly she delights me but I
know so little about the natives
her sources so to speak
Hollister at that time was a town of four thousand
becoming a Freudian deviant in method more than
theory.

~Paul Corman-Roberts

Abigail Mouat

Abigail Mouat is 35 years old and lives in Gainesville, FL. She has been writing poems and short stories ever since she can remember and it has been more than a means of expression to her; it has become a way of life. She works for the local utility company in her hometown and has one daughter.

Here, There Be Dragons

here,
there be dragons.
off the map,
i fall into a no man's land
filled with dangerous awe.

i have
circumnavigated the globe,
tamed the wild native
in me;
i have
fought disease, pestilence and
drought,
death and starvation.
my cross-cultural education
is complete.

i am
invaded,
domesticated and,
finally, integrated.
there are
no more new countries
to see.

~Abigail E. Mouat

Poseidon

my trident is tossed
and it lands
with a thunk
in the gilded silt
beneath the ocean.

i smash the glass
of the waves
with my fist
and scatter them
away from my reflection

this tempest
of my jealousy
will make those
without sea-legs
green like me.

oh anger! rage!
those pearls of
irrational fear
they have bejeweled me
once again.

~Abigail E. Mouat

Woman

i do not want
to be a man
though
as a woman
i inhabit a body
that has never been
my own.

first my mother's
to bathe and
clothe;
she held me
to soothe herself,
a little
immortality.

then men;
passed me
along
they always wanting
a share of
what i possess
unlocking the legs
but rarely
the heart.

then friends,
who strive
to take their fill
remove the
remoteness
for however short
a time.

and then
my child's,
she consumes me
from within
forming under the
rib,
more flesh and
bone.

finally death;
he takes what's left
which is,
granted,
not much
but by then
does it matter?

perhaps
it may be better
to be a man;
to have one body
inviolate
to pursue
the emptiness
and withdraw
when satisfied.

~Abigail E. Mouat

Tom Watts

Tom Watts is a 28 year old part-time chef and full-time writer living in South-West London. He spends his time writing, drinking and fighting the good fight. His work has appeared in Killpoet, In Between Hangovers, Remark Poetry, and decomP Magazine.

You Can Use Your Breathing as a Weapon.

You
Can use
Your breathing as a weapon
A huff
A puff
And
I'll know
That you're
Grizzly bear angry

You're sad
When you sigh
Like a million
Freight trains slowing

Surprise
Sounds like
Airbrakes on
A cross-country coach
Cutting through a circus

And
If I listen
Real
Close
I can hear
When I'm getting lucky

~Tom Watts

I Put the Cork in the Bottle and Stop the Sound.

Tonight
There's a baton
In the wine
That's conducting me

So many
Mistakes
In the timing
And the tempo
Tetchy sections
Of the Orchestra
Spit notes
At lit cigarettes

There are
Broken bows
Drums rolls
For nothing

The wine
Being innocent
Does not know
Its effect

It sits
In the glass
Waiting
Whilst I steal
The silver
From the
Fold-lined
Tablecloth
And order lobster
I cannot pay for

I want to go home.

I put the cork in the bottle and stop the sound.

~Tom Watts

Medication.

I see you
Shuffling along
The ward Corridors
A dressing gown
Wrapped round nothing

When I look at you
I see
The place where I work
With the lights off
The power down

Blinking red dots
In the darkness

The edge
Of stainless steel
Work surfaces
Cutting the darkness
Like the sleeping knives
In the racks

Familiar
Like when you dream of home
But in your heart
You know it's nothing like it

Fragile as my grandma's handwriting
On birthday cards
Placed like dead cheques
In a box on a shelf

~Tom Watts

Shawn Misener

Shawn Misener lives in Michigan and likes panic attacks, violently romantic affairs, incoherent speech, and music that makes your hips move uncontrollably.

Japanese Miniskirts Under the Ishtar Terra

exiting the pub I look up
into a rare clear night
and see Venus in detail
crouched up next to earth

it seems as though someone has
picked you up, Venus
and parked you next to us

I feel woozy and think
oh shit-
somebody must have spiked my drink

I should sit down on the tiny grass hill
cozying up to the pub
and breathe a little
then brave looking up again

+++

suddenly
the door slams open
exhuming two tiny Japanese women
hysterically laughing in black miniskirts
holding each other up

their drunken ruckus trails off
when one of them looks up
and points to Venus-
then faints

the other screams and runs down the street

I want to look again
but my eyes won't open
I know Venus has swallowed the night sky
without good reason

+++

suddenly
the professors emerge from the bar
in a cloud of masculine cackle
they too are silenced by the sight of Venus
and possibly the unconscious Japanese woman in a miniskirt

only a second of silence then they pipe up
with sheer excitement
I hear them jumping up and down
I hear mysterious words couched
between oooohs and aaaahs

great words, actually:
Ishtar Terra
Aphrodite Terra
Lakshmi Planum
Maxwell Montes

Could it be?
Maxwell Montes was a great friend of mine-
as children we used to chase red squirrels
and pretend to be Hulk Hogan or Jake the Snake

then he ran away in sixth grade
and was never seen again

+++

I stand and look at the men
who all have immaculate grey beards
and I don't see Maxwell Montes amongst them

yet they keep repeating his name,
pointing fervently toward Venus

was Maxwell descending from the sky?
is that him, naked and with long hair,
floating graciously to earth on a *giant clam shell*?

+++

I tilt nervously to the sky, but he isn't there
neither is Venus
but the Japanese woman remains
stylistically sprawled across the sidewalk

the professors are nowhere to be seen
and I think again that somebody messed with my drink

~Shawn Misener

Spring Meditation

The morning sinks into sponge.
The coffee sponge that I am,
I go for a third cup.

Smoke curls the air
but I have nothing to smoke.

The distant nearby
hum of whirring machinery
keeps me in good company.

Cars on the road shimmer with doppler,
which sounds transcendent at the moment.

Thoughts are sticky and hang together
like a room full of flypaper
with no open space for new flies.

Sit within myself,
that's what the dream monk told me to do.
I remember now, even though I knew it all along.

~Shawn Misener

Ventricle Blues

How far away is space?

To restate:
How much space is between
us and space?

To inquire more personally:
How much space is between
you and I?

To be slightly icky:
How much space is between
my fourth and fifth vertebrae?

Is it more space than yours?
Because you hunch sometimes.

***

Look at the stars with me tonight.
I know where there's a secret supernova.

I know where there's a blues record
in which Muddy Waters moans
about spaces in the heart.

You'll hear it when we tune in
to the hidden supernova.

~Shawn Misener

Charlie Chapman

Charlie Chapman has been published in various UK magazines, the most recent being Poetry Cornwall and In Between Hangovers. She has a chapbook coming out as chapbook #5 at Cat Scan Press. She lives in the woods with the poet Paul Tristram and their son Harvey where she writes poetry and makes babies. Their second son Rowan is due in July.

The Witches Tree

Alone in the middle of the field,
the great witches tree stands beautifully.
Majestic and imposing for all to behold.
The hollow, lightning struck trunk full of bluebells.
No leaves grow anymore
but there is more beauty in this one dead tree,
than in a forest of green.

~Charlie Chapman

Jelly Babies And Sausage Rolls

I'm four months pregnant
and it's freezing out.
My man is on a mission
all the way to the 24 hour Tesco.
I wont give in
and he won't get any.
Not until I get what I want,
Jelly babies (room temperature)
and sausage rolls (hot).
It's 2am but I don't care.
I've been dreaming about it,
a bite of one
then a bite of the other.
I'll make it up to him later
but for now
Jelly babies and sausage rolls
are all that matter.

~Charlie Chapman

Calm down love.

He's on the edge of his seat,
watching the different people flash by.
He doesn't agree with their words
so he swears and curses them away.
The controls are in his hand
giggling I break his concentration,
looking from the TV to him I ask
"Have you got Tourette's again, love?"

~Charlie Chapman

Rebecca Schumejda

Rebecca Schumejda lives in New York's Hudson Valley. She is the author of two chapbooks "The Tear Duct of the Storm" published by Green Bean Press and "Dream Big, Work Harder" published by sunnyoutside press. She received her MA in poetics from San Francisco State University.

Castles

Just a combination of
damp sand, time, mounting
frustration with the tide and
my father planting tulip bulbs
upside down in storm clouds.

Because nothing and everything
makes sense, at night, I listen
as the world erodes the shores
of my sanity, one petal at a time.

My body, a peninsula, holds onto
ghost shadows. I never saw
a dead man until my father,
now I can't see much else.

Excuse my husband's
snoring, the wind, the rain and
the mistakes I will hide from
my children.

The tower too thin at the base,
held steady by stubborn hands
just long enough for my father
to critique, crumbled out of his
sight like his own heart.

Who will rebuild the towers?
Who will turn the tulips around?

~Rebecca Schumejda

Six Months from Now
For Mark

Afraid to push into me, you
go downstairs to read the paper.
In the kitchen's dull light,
the shadows on the walls
become a city of uninvited guests.
We'll have to get use to
not being alone anymore.

When you read, the scars
above each of your eyes
crease, the thin line between
then and now, where the shadows
of who you were, push in
and out like the tide
and heavy thoughts, unafraid.

Don't tell me not to worry;
I've witnessed the tide steal
a child from his mother,
the stretch marks left on
abandoned shores, your eyes
in the shadow of thought,
so distant, so unrecognizable

~Rebecca Schumejda

Dreaming You Up

Your father
dreamt you up,
imagined you a girl
of eleven with
sandy-blonde hair
and blue eyes,
silent and sullen
like his own.

Petrified of a girl-child,
I only dream
of past-lives
people and places
that could have been
familiar
in contrast to those
that are.

Lately, my mother
makes sense,
the way she always seemed
distant and dutiful;
chasing purpose
around the house
with broom
and dustpan;
scrubbing reason
with steel wool
and desperation.

How I hate
the spotlessness;
everything sparkling,
folded or tidied,

except me.
Oh, how my tantrums
drove her mad.
How I would run
outside naked
and squealing
whenever she hung
the laundry
out to dry.

Am I wrong
for not dreaming
you up? Instead,
I admire how
this morning's
salmon and violet bans
distort the valley's sky
like stretch marks.

~Rebecca Schumejda

Justin Hyde

Justin Hyde lives in Iowa. He can be contacted at
jjjjhyde@yahoo.com

//the crackhead//

tells me
he and his father
caught chubs
out of a creek
behind the airport
but he never could put a worm
on the hook
cause he'd imagine himself
as the worm
how much
it must have hurt.
says
there was a pregnant
street-woman
at the bus stop today
he heard her
talking to a friend
she was craving ice cream
he bought her a drumstick
from the walgreens
across the street
she started crying.
his hands shake constantly
he pushes his finger
into his head
above his left eye
says he can feel another migraine
coming on.
mr justin
(that's what he calls me,
i'm his parole officer)
you done told me
you was an atheist

somethin awful
must have happened to you
to think that way,
i don't expect you to tell me what
but i'll help you see
yet,
he smiles
showing the top row of empty teeth
holds out
his hand.

~Justin Hyde

//angry black kid//

4:42 mile
state runner up
freshman year of high school
started slinging rock
for the vice lords
caught his first number at fifteen
five years probation
contingent on completing
the work release program
in the back conference room
sitting across from each other
said i was singling him out
why was i riding his shit?
i'm enforcing the rules
i don't play favorites
you were given a directive
to go to your room
you ignored it
slammed his fists on the table
this is fucking bullshit
racist motherfucking co's
went out hollering into the main floor
week later
didn't come back
from his job at mcdonald's
picked up five days later
selling to an undercover
judge imposed the full nickle
boxcared two more for absconding
i follow him in prison on the computer
been raped
maced
had the dog drag him from his cell
scheduled to be out cold
on the streets
in less than a year
then what?

~*Justin Hyde*

anytime, i said, anytime you need anything at all

crew chief
at long john silver's - -

dedicated
to his children - -

liked to play pool - -

obituary
goes on -

mentioning nothing
about hanging by his neck
from an iron truss
at a construction site,

the conversations
in my office
about the need
to always take his depakote,

or the day
three weeks ago,

discharging him from parole
i put my personal cell number
in his hand.

~Justin Hyde

Duane Honeydew

Duane Honeydew, master of indecent arts, has rested his unholy claws in Alaska, Norway, the coldest corners of the universe, Syracuse University, and Montana. Currently lives amongst wolves in Northern Wisconsin. Has published bad poems in countless literary publications, most now defunct. Last collection, "Methinks Myself A Crudly One," was printed by Fat Candiru Press.

WINGS TORN FROM HOPE'S FEATHERED CORPSE

Vultures grin, perched on both sides of the jury.
Erase the possibility of innocence, gentle people.
Read the words on my razor-thin lips.
Damnation is the only acceptable punishment.
I sing the body electric, strapped tightly to a chair.
Can't you see the evil in their young faces?
The judge strangles a bird shot down from the sky.

~Duane Honeydew

TRUE STORIES OF A MEDIA MASSACRE

Jail the witches. Hell, kill 'em at the same time.
Use your hands next time. Less blood.
Sell me your soul, I'll sell you a helluva story.
Turn Court TV louder honey, that stuff's crazy.
Ignore the fanged creature under the table.
Cell rats grin as the weeping boy approaches.
Earthquakes have more compassion for victims.

~Duane Honeydew

TWIST THE KNIFE IN THE BLADDER OF MADNESS

Kill the hummingbird, and kill it good.
Not since 'Nam have I been this happy.
Ultraviolence? Flavor of the day, monsieur.
Can you smell the blood under my nails?
Ketchup stains scream on my plaid underwear.
Lunch break was full of screams again.
Every dead man has his day to rot.

~Duane Honeydew

Christopher Robin

Christopher Robin is the editor of Zen Baby zine and the author of a book of poetry entitled Freaky Mumbler's Manifesto. Recent work can be found at www.literaryrevolution.com. He lives in Santa Cruz, CA.

Who We Kill

The mentally ill
Who wave water pistols
The blacks who wave wallets
And can't surrender fast enough
The animals that weren't cute enough
The animals that made the mistake
Of being born delicious…
The trannies that can't hide
The mistake of being born wrong…
The self-taught publishers
Who overflow the toilets
In the Borders bathroom
The lone poet
Who furiously walks the streets
Thinking maybe around the next corner
The world will show me some light
The service workers who spend their pay
In the local bars
And their imaginations on satellite dishes
The prisoners who make our goods for no pay…
The muddy trumpet players
With their songs of drowning
On america's rooftops….
The musty bookstores of my childhood
With shelves that went on forever
And kept me from the taunting of schoolmates…
The roadside fruit stands
We passed on our way to Christmas in Soledad-
The high rents here will send my friends away:
The potters who can't sell their pots
Musicians whose notes are out of time
Poets who can't sell their revolutionary poem
For a crust of bread from a birds beak

We're not the chosen ones
And nobody's buying anyway
So get on SSI or find a better hustle,
A barn, a roach-infested shoebox
At the El Palomar
Or maybe a room at El Centro
Where they didn't find the body
And the fluids dripped through the floor
Into the restaurant below…
And there's always that old standby
The bridge behind Denny's
Where I used to drink coffee
Crawl into my bag
And scribble poetry onto the concrete wall
Not waiting for a publisher
Just the light of day

~Christopher Robin

A HOT CUP OF SANITY
WHICH EVERYONE DESERVES

Everyone wants coffee
And everyone deserves it
But some folks can't have any
Because they've been 86ED
You *gotta* hold it together
No matter how much you talk to yourself
While walking the streets
When someone else shows up in your view
Stop doing it
Let this little test be a measure of your sanity
I do it all the time
I'm *really* careful
I tilt my eyes to the sky
I'm kicking stones
Furiously scribbling
furiously mumbling…
I am saying A LOT of things please believe
But I still get to have COFFEE
I've got a few dollars
I've stayed out of the madhouse
My social worker only shows up every six months
My friends all have pretty good hygiene…
But it is really a fine fine line….
So if you are sitting in the café
In the middle of a weekday afternoon
And one of you has snakes in her bra
And one of you has already drunk a bottle of wine
count yourselves among the lucky
Raise a cup of that bitter, delicious drink
of complete and total sanity
Drink unmolested
Stay as long as you like
Leave a tip

~Christopher Robin   170

SLOWTIME RACE TO NOWHERE

Told I'm slow
I move at half the world's speed
2 sizes
2 big
black Converse
stay
2 cups of coffee
ahead
of the insults
one good arm
for
waving
at trains
my best eye
avoiding
stepping on
used needles
and layin my pennies
down
on the track
leg muscles taut
head down
in
hood
for the revolution
we'll all be walking
and eyes on the ground
now I practice
collecting discarded fruit from the trees
which I happily eat
as if I am the lone survivor
of a suburban apocalypse
you'll see them on TV
outdoing us all:

the blind climb Mount Everest
amputees play the piano
the 'locked-in' invent their own alphabet
don't know what excuse I have
for a guy stuck in the 4th grade
you gotta be a genius of something
but I figure
they'll kill you either way
with a glassy stare
or run you over
when you're peering
into the gutters
of your neighborhood
clothing in shreds
frantic for a spark
anything that can still catch fire…
all *I'm* doing is telling secrets
telling on myself
and telling on you
I hate Oprah anyway

   ~Christopher Robin

Debbie Kirk

Debbie Kirk has been in the small press off and on for 7 years. She's had 5 chapbooks published and been published in such magazines as: Zygote in my Coffee, Impetus, Remark, Open Wide Magazine, and Mystery Island. She's gone to every benefit for the WM3 that she could possibly attend, it's something close close close to her heart, and she is flattered to be a part of this anthology. She can be reached at sinnncity66613@yahoo.com

5 bucks on Micheline

Baby,
I'm glad you can still taste me on your lips...
Can still smell my pussy on your fingers.

but I was in New Orleans with Jack Micheline
he had some paintings
and I had a boom swagger boom
laying down some lines
that resembled webs

and we got a bet goin'
to see who the real hustler is
And, I'm feeling lucky....

So, could you use your fucking hands
and let me go back to sleep?

~Debbie Kirk
Published by Poems For all Press mini poem series 2004

An experiment regarding how many times I can get away with saying "Bukowski" in a single poem

People often tell me that I write like Bukowski.
I usually hit 'em back with:
"I don't write like Bukowski, But I probably fuck like Bukowski."
Almost anyone can be a drunk
And dabble in the words.

Neither candy bars nor prostitutes
Were cited as his muse.
Bukowski simply had it,
And when he left he took it with him
Deep in the dirt
In the real underground.

No one will ever be able to write like Bukowski, it's true.
But I smile as I put a tampon in my pocket and head to the bathroom.
Back and belly on fire from cramps
And I think:
"Bukowski wouldn't have ever been able to write like me either."

~Debbie Kirk

Maybe I should have been a child molester

I grew up in foster care
In Arkansas
I had black nail polish
Combat boots
Wore black everyday
And had purple hair

People made jokes about me
As kids do in high school
They called me a Devil worshiper
When I'd walk up to hang
They'd joke that they knew
Debbie was coming
Because the weather was getting warmer

If there had been a death
Of a child
With no evidence
I might have been lucky enough
To be playing cards
With Damien Echols right now.

But no one dies
Ironically, a tragedy?
I think those kids
Could have done more
For the world than me
Sometimes

And wish I would have been framed
For the infamous yogurt shop murders

But I wasn't

I feel like a prisoner
In my home a lot
Since the rape

But I have decided
I have to go out
Into the fucked up world
And do enough for
All four of us

Because I unfortunately
Don't see justice
In the crystal ball
For these kids.

~Debbie Kirk

David S. Pointer

David S. Pointer previously served as a United States Marine Military Policeman. Currently, he has poetry forthcoming in "Blue Collar Review," "Illya's Honey," "Nerve Cowboy," and "The American Dissident."

West Memphis Three Murders

West Memphis is one big truck stop...
-Dee Canaly

Maybe there's a
prisoner somewhere
lighting cigarettes
from an altered
electrical outlet
offering to tell
the other inmates
the unauthorized
tale of three eight
year old boys in the
West Memphis murders
in exchange for a
shampoo bottle full
of orange peel wine,
shop shank, or maybe
he's not one prisoner
but two free men eating
at the Sugar Bucket
diner-both having poached
eggs with pork bits stewed
in milk making plans to
overhaul their old mobile
meth lab that really had a
fondness for the proverbial
sweet hitchhiker even when
it was three young boys on
bikes that could be absorbed
into their short party on
wheels rolling slow past
Robin Hood Hills greenery.

~David S. Pointer

The Unheard Echo
of Damien Echols

There's a certain
terror in knowing
DNA tests can be
denied like early
parole, can be
turned away from
testifying in the
open courtroom
like witnesses, can
be made to bear
false witness against
self or someone else:
A convicted person
can wait so long
for DNA tests that
they start wishing for
the Lincoln Continental
of lethal injections
administered by a
qualified medical
doctor or medical
professional not
an alcoholic warden
stumbling around
with a size 18 needle
not even a new
nurse's aide wearing
a floor-grade smile.

~*David S. Pointer*

Deep Legal:
Look Again

The evidence bin was
empty. The Police and
Prosecutor's answering
machines were over
full with mayoral office
murmurations of outrage
and insistence that the
culprit be caught. Sometimes
a complete lack of evidence
is all you need-after all-
nothing charges the air
in a tourist town like
triple child murder soon
to commingle with triple
teen convictions, and
a case that won't scrub
clean, or stay out of the
scripts of Hollywood types
asking that the agony, and
untouchable be reautopsied,
examined, and unclouded,
amongst the grief and three
small granite headstones.

~David S. Pointer

Brian Necessary

Brian Necessary has been writing since 2002. His hobbies/interests are ghost hunting, cryptozoology, collecting swords, daggers, and dragons.

CRITICIZED

Been wrongly accused by society
For not fittin in the standard of society
I'm just a outcast of society
Just for being who I am

I listen to different music than you
I look and dress different than you
I just have different interest than you
But I am happy being who I am

Because I'm different in your eyes
You just judge me without knowin me
You are just scared of me
The bible says judge not lest ye be judge

You have convicted me
Not on evidence but on fear
Because I don't fit into your society
You look down on me

I am being condemned
I am servin a life sentence
Goin by you I'm goin to burn in hell
Cause in yours eyes I am evil

Anything that you don't like
Or you don't understand
You right away says it evil
It is from the devil

You just fear it cause it's different
You will label it evil
You want to destroy it
Before anyone else can see it

Just give me a chance
And get to know me
You will see I am not evil
I am just a person like you

Don't be quick to judge me
Just let me be me
Accept me for who I am
Don't try to change me

Then you will finally see
That I am a not a evil monster
You will see I am good person
Just someone who is misunderstood

~Brian Necessary

I WILL ALWAYS REMEMBER YOU

As the tears fall from our eyes,
We look at you through our fears,
We say our final goodbyes,
As we shed the last of our tears....

You are so dearly missed,
And how we miss seeing your face,
We walk with a different pace,
But you're in such a better place

The day I kissed you goodbye,
was the longest, coldest, darkest,
and the most painful day of my life

I know that you're in heaven now,
an with a smile you're lookin down,
I hope that everyday,
somehow I've made you proud.
The LORD had to take you back,
but I wish he'd have gave me time,
to whisper to you,
the feelings in my mind

All that I have left of you,
is memories and never ending love,
I cherish every short second with you,
I'll give you more when I get to come up.

You'll always be in my heart,
My love will always be true,
I will always.......remember you
Inside you're always here with me,
In everything I do, and..
I will always.......remember you
    ~Brian Necessary

I JUST WANNA GO BACK TO MY HOME

There's this place that I call home,
Seems forever....that I've been gone...
That place takes all my pain away,
I'm just ready...to go home... today.

Memories they seem to give away,
they hide this life I live today,
I believe my mind has gone astray,
I'm just ready...to go home ...today.

(and) I'm so tired...of living this way
I'm just ready...to go home...2 day

I know that my day's coming soon,
I need to make my peace anyway
my heart wants to see all through the grey,
I just want...to go home...today

Are you gonna celebrate my life?
Please don't cry we all live to die
Pray the LORD will take me home tonight,
Pray the LORD will make it all alright
Are you gonna go on with you're life,
He only takes us when the time is right,
Pray the LORD will take me home tonight
I know that the LORD will make it alright,
I know that the LORD will make it right

I just wanna go back...to my home...
The only place that makes happy
I just wanna go back....to my home
The only place where I can breathe
I just wanna go back...to my home
I just want...to go home...alone...

~Brian Necessary

Dennis L. Roberson
a.k.a.
Untouchable

Dennis L. Roberson lives in southern California. He is currently in the Army and serving in Iraq. He wishes to God bless all the families that have loved ones protecting our nation and to the people who support us. They are the Supermen and women, the driving force and the inspiration of every one of the fellow troops on the frontline. He can be contacted at www.myspace.com/airbornewolf

MATERIAL SHIT

THE WORLD'S MADE OF MATERIAL THINGS
MOST OF WHICH IS JUST LIES.
WE BELIEVE IN MATERIAL SHIT
BUT WE BELIEVE TO GET BY.
YEAH, I GO TO STRIP CLUBS,
MOST LIKE TO ASK ME WHY.
I TELL THEM TO SEE THE DANCERS,
THROW THEM A FEW DOLLARS
TO SEE THEM GET BY.
I TELL THEM GO TO COLLEGE
GET OUT OF THE LIFE.
RAISE YOUR KIDS RIGHT
THEY DON'T LIKE TO CRY.
IN THIS DAY OF AGE,
AN AGE OF VIOLENCE AND CRIME,
WE BELIEVE IN GUNS AND KNIVES
INSTEAD OF HOW HARD THE CHILDREN TRY.
THEY GONNA LEARN FROM EXPERIENCE,
THEY GONNA LIVE THEIR LIVES.
AS HARD AS IT IS TO SAY,
SOMEDAY, WE ALL GONNA DIE.
SO HOLD ON TO YOUR MATERIAL LOVE,
ITS WHAT GETS US BY.

~Dennis L. Roberson

LARGER THAN LIFE

THE LARGEST THING IN LIFE IS LIFE ITSELF
SO TO BE LARGER THAN LIFE, LET YOUR PROBLEMS
BE SOLVED, SITUATIONS BE DELT
THE REALIZATION OF HESITATION,
PROCRASTINATION, PERSECUTION, AND
TEMPTATION, BRINGS JUSTIFICATION TO SELF.
WHO OTHER TO REALIZE WHO ELSE THAN ONE'S
SELF
WHEN YOU FINALLY REALIZE YOU'RE ON TOP,
DON'T LET ANYONE OR ANYTHING KNOCK YOU
DOWN A NOTCH.
IF THEY DO ITS NOT YOUR'S BUT THEIR OWN IMAGE
THEY BLOTCH 'CAUSE OF THE LIES THEY BOUGHT.
HELP THEM REMEMBER TO LET THEIR OWN
PROBLEMS BE SOLVED,
HELP THEM SNATCH THE JUSTIFICATION THAT'S
DELT,
TO THEM YOU'LL BE LARGER THAN LIFE ITSELF.

~Dennis L. Roberson

Over da Edge

-As I sit here waitin, contemplatin
-On what I do wrong,
-I sit here hatin and marinatin on the words of my song
-Eatin away my perception, conception
-Of spirit, mind, and health
-Askin myself,
-What the hell it takes to earn prosperity and wealth
-Or to rid my life of these problems i delt,
-Or the problems of the ones I love
-My cousin, at the age of 21
-Already has a daughter at the age of 1
-She relyin on the stamps she gets once a month,
-To put food on the table, or die by the gun
-Or my uncles....
- Listen, I love you to death
-But it kills me sometimes, for what you put in your body and head
-One sold his own son's furniture just to get a fix in his bed
-We found him two weeks later, in an alley, half dead
-Shit makes me wonder what pushes a nigga over da edge

~Dennis L. Roberson

Gloriane

Age: 30 - Gloriane is moody mess who likes to spastically dance to her Sex Pistols and Operation Ivy record albums around the house. She cannot spell properly and relies on the computer Spellchecker way too much. She is a semi-gullible goof who loves Bret Easton Ellis and Kate Chopin books. Gloriane has contributed to a few poetry book collaborations including, FROM A COMMON SPRING 1&2, THE VIRTUAL CHEMISTS 1&2, and various online publications. All Gloriane's book collaborations are on **Lulu.com** and she encourages supporting the underground poetry culture. She currently resides in Anaheim, California with husband Jeremy and 112lb black lab, (who thinks he's Shih Tzu) Lucky.

Web page: http://www.myspace.com/88917299

Pathetic paranoid psychosis
Hordes of hell
Ridiculous rash
Rampant roar
Larynx bloodbath
Eardrums implode
Canals convulse
An inner storm
Tubes shredded
Vibrations discord
Cartilage kaput
Wax, fluid, and hairs are soot
Auditory ossicles liquidated
Cochlea mutilated
An unbalanced Beethoven with no music experience created

~Gloriane

The baboon of bad behavior that is bundled up in you needs to
buckle down
Can you sack the sorrow or put it on simmer
A lack of joy in your life has jumbled your head
And you cannot keep yourself completely conducted
The waves of your temperament torment
My Nervous System begins to change shape
Migraines maneuver up my membrane
Morphing me into a demented Acupuncturist
Planning preposterous plots to poke pins in your skin to
attempt to puncture the proper parts
That could:
A. Result in revitalization and relaxation with permeate peace,
or
B. Accidental death

~Gloriane

I suppose I just slowly move
What do I have to lose?
I have already lost a lot
My stomach remains a permanent knot
I have seen 8 or more go underground
My heart will forever wear a black shroud
I can't interpret the intense loss
That your body goes through when smothering in moss
My hands trembling
Thoughts dismembering
Panic attacks
Catastrophic distress
Trying to grip
In the foggy mist
The horrendous blitz
Of life's unpredictable twists

~*Gloriane*

Michael W. Johnson

Michael W. Johnson lives @ the KY/TN border and has been writing words "artistically" since the early 90's. He has many books and such @ www.lulu.com/loserland or www.myspace.com/fauxpas23 . He strives to always fight against the narrow-minded views the world seems determined to uphold. Fearing and hating that which is different from us will always lead to downfall.

Media Junkie

I killed 63 people today
With my controller anyway
I sang 9 songs
About homicide without repent
I watched 2 movies
With a total body count of 104
Does this feed my instinct to murder?
No, it merely fills spaces of time
Violent images in media are the witches of today
Prosecuted and slandered by insecure conservatives
Who spend their lives pointing fingers
At the unaccountable and innocent
If your child is becoming a Satan spawn
Don't blame it on Marilyn Manson
Don't blame it on anyone
Instead, try to control and correct the problem
That's the real issue

So long have we sacrificed the scapegoats
Protests and petitions, bans and ratings
And never cure the dysfunction
Allowing it to fester and explode
Most killers have no healthy outlet
No way to satisfy their appetite
The boredom and frustration eventually overpowers them
So at the next dead body found
Don't accuse me and other media junkies
We'll be on the sofa
Ripping someone's torso in half on the TV screen

~Michael W. Johnson

Biased Much?

Look at her
An anti-social girl
Pensive and meditating
Obviously with a hidden agenda
How can she wear black year 'round?
Does she sacrifice?
Is she in a cult?
Obviously there's something going on
No normal person
Dresses, talks, acts, lives
The way that she does
Obviously she cuts herself
Does all kinds of drugs
And sleeps with anyone
She is a loner in darkness
What use is she to society?
Not a part of the solution, must be a problem
Not part of the wheel
Must be rolled over and crushed
Never be productive and functional
She is subculture
Subclass, subhuman.

~Michael W. Johnson

Stereos Play Music, They Don't Type

Must I always be defined
By what I wear?
Must you always pigeonhole me
Because I am different?

Pop culture will not
Dictate my personality

This lion may be cowardly
Or he may rip your damn throat out
This tin man may have a heart of gold
Or could be the coldest son of a bitch around
This scarecrow may be dumb
Or perhaps is only allowing that misleading interpretation

Remember the book/cover rule
I'm not who you think
It'll only take a little time
And tolerance
For you to find that out.

~Michael W. Johnson

Misti Rainwater-Lites

Misti Rainwater-Lites cannot watch CNN without screaming expletives at the screen. Read her blogs at http://ebulliencepress.blogspot.com. Buy her books at http://www.lulu.com/ebulliencepress.

Anorexic Rant

blah blah blah with sandpaper tongue
america feeds its young to grinning jaws
that smack and ask for back taxes
and freshly grown balls
america does not
want me intact
america wants me chewable
in fruity star shaped vitamins
america wants my fingers and toes
for an appetizer
america wants my ovaries
sunny side up
america wants my butt
with plenty of butter
america wants my cunt juices
sweetly flowing
calorie free
america wants my head
on a gleaming silver platter
america wants to gnaw
on my bones
america the innocent puppy dog
wagging its tail
all the way to the market
america here i am
your broken bread girl
stales bits and pieces
to dunk in your overflowing
goblet of wine
here is my heart america
eat this in remembrance of me
here is my resume
my beauty pageant tiara

my rapture and tribulation nightmares
my snoopy diary
my rotten teeth
my anxious brain
my mangled spirit
my damaged hair
my tits
my acne
take this, america
this is my hope
may it be a rock firmly lodged
in your cocaine gullet
choke on me, america
i want to see you turn blue
i want to see you dangle
from a tree
like your cotton pickin
gospel singin
sour fruit slaves
look at me, america
look at me and be ashamed
i want your face
to turn redder
than the blood on your graceful
piano playin hands
boo, america
boo from a random ghost
one of your forgotten odd numbers
i am rattling my rusty chains
frozen in your basement
with the ice cream sandwiches
look at me, america
look at me and be very afraid
i want your face to turn whiter
than the bones of your dead presidents

and by the book bankers
whiter than an actors teeth
whiter than a trophy wife's
bleached asshole
whiter than the skin
of your class pet
go disco, america
go crazy rainbow light extravaganza
go electric
go spastic
like the innocent people
who could not afford decent representation
and fried in your chair

go to jail, america
go to jail and visit
your illiterate single mom on welfare raised
tattooed criminals
go to hell, america
the hell that is your prison system
visit damien echols on death row in arkansas
look into his eyes and beg
for his forgiveness
look in the mirror, america
see how ridiculous you are
your hair is a mass of writhing
hissing snakes
your eyes are bugged
your ribs are showing
you have become a grotesque caricature
you are over the hill but still dressed
in a raggedy ann costume
no one believes you
put yourself to good use, america
chew me up some more

validate me with your greedy fangs
chew with cold precision
chew chew chew
your chosen loser
then shit me out
your starry anus
flush me down the toilet, america
watch me swirl
merrily merrily merrily merrily
another forgotten dream

~Misti Rainwater-Lites

American Xmas 2006

Some of us lucky bitches are getting diamonds for Christmas
from our loving husbands.
Some of us luckier bitches are getting good sex for xmas
from our generous husbands.
Some of us are not in America this Christmas. Some of us are
in Iraq losing our arms and legs.
Ho ho ho. Blood glows bright red like Rudolph's nose.
Some of us are getting eviction notices for xmas.
Some of us are ending our year with a bang.
America does not want us. Goodbye, America. Our suicide
note is our brains on the walls of our studio apartments.
But don't lose heart. Some of us are getting big fat bonuses for
Christmas.
Some of us will go to the ballet and then eat sushi and drink
sake with our rich witty friends.
The Christmas tree in Rockefeller Center still shines bright
white hope for Wall Street geniuses and their plastic surgery
beautiful wives. Not everyone is hungry or disenfranchised.
Some of us are fat and sassy this Christmas.
Jesus loves us more than he loves you.
Jesus has blessed us with big houses, new cars, smiling cherubs
and little people lining up to kiss our successful asses.
It doesn't matter that Jesus wasn't really born in December.
It doesn't matter that Jesus was a Pisces.
It doesn't matter that the Christians stole Christmas from the
Pagans.
It doesn't matter that there is nothing remotely Christian or
charitable about spending tons of money on gifts for people
who already have more than they need and putting pressure on
loved ones with a wish list a mile long.
Celebrate, goddamn it.
Drink your eggnog.

Eat your fruitcake.
Smile pretty for the camera.
Let it snow let it glow let it show the world
that Americans are the most blessed people
on this green and blue planet.
Lucky Americans.
Happy Americans.
The rest of the world does not hate America.
That is just a rumor.

~Misti Rainwater-Lites

CAGE RAGE DENIAL

livin' large
like cleopatra's barge
big ass house
big ass cars
big ass baby
bouncin' and smilin'
for snap happy cameras
we love the cage
bars don't bother us none
this is the fairy tale
we sucked our thumbs to
this is happily ever after
swimmin' in debt
it's a sea of freedom
star spangled and spacious
we're not drownin'
we're wavin'
at the bums on the beach
who only wish
they had it
this good

~Misti Rainwater-Lites

www.ingramcontent.com/pod-product-compliance
Lightning Source LLC
Chambersburg PA
CBHW030928090426
42737CB00007B/357